IS THE OPM DATA BREACH
THE TIP OF THE ICEBERG?

JOINT HEARING

BEFORE THE

SUBCOMMITTEE ON OVERSIGHT &
SUBCOMMITTEE ON RESEARCH AND TECHNOLOGY
COMMITTEE ON SCIENCE, SPACE, AND
TECHNOLOGY
HOUSE OF REPRESENTATIVES

ONE HUNDRED FOURTEENTH CONGRESS

FIRST SESSION

July 8, 2015

Serial No. 114–28

Printed for the use of the Committee on Science, Space, and Technology

Available via the World Wide Web: http://science.house.gov

U.S. GOVERNMENT PUBLISHING OFFICE

97–568PDF   WASHINGTON : 2016

For sale by the Superintendent of Documents, U.S. Government Publishing Office
Internet: bookstore.gpo.gov   Phone: toll free (866) 512–1800; DC area (202) 512–1800
Fax: (202) 512–2104   Mail: Stop IDCC, Washington, DC 20402–0001

(II)

CONTENTS

July 8, 2015

	Page
Witness List	2
Hearing Charter	3

Opening Statements

Statement by Representative Barbara Comstock, Chairwoman, Subcommittee on Research, Committee on Science, Space, and Technology, U.S. House of Representatives 7
    Written Statement 8
Statement by Representative Daniel Lipinski, Ranking Minority Member, Subcommittee on Research, Committee on Science, Space, and Technology, U.S. House of Representatives 9
    Written Statement 11
Statement by Representative Barry Loudermilk, Chairman, Subcommittee on Oversight, Committee on Science, Space, and Technology, U.S. House of Representatives 12
    Written Statement 13
Statement by Representative Donald S. Beyer, Jr., Ranking Minority Member, Subcommittee on Oversight, Committee on Science, Space, and Technology, U.S. House of Representatives 14
    Written Statement 16
Statement by Representative Lamar S. Smith, Chairman, Committee on Science, Space, and Technology, U.S. House of Representatives 17
    Written Statement 18

Witnesses:

Mr. Michael R. Esser, Assistant Inspector General for Audits, Office of Personnel Management
    Oral Statement 19
    Written Statement 22
Mr. David Snell, Director, Federal Benefits Service Department, National Active and Retired Federal Employees Association
    Oral Statement 33
    Written Statement 35
Dr. Charles Romine, Director, Information Technology Laboratory, National Institute of Standards and Technology
    Oral Statement 42
    Written Statement 44
Mr. Gregory Wilshusen, Director, Information Security Issues, U.S. Government Accountability Office
    Oral Statement 50
    Written Statement 52
Discussion 78

Appendix I: Answers to Post-Hearing Questions

Mr. Michael R. Esser, Assistant Inspector General for Audits, Office of Personnel Management 96

Page

Mr. David Snell, Director, Federal Benefits Service Department, National Active and Retired Federal Employees Association 100

Dr. Charles Romine, Director, Information Technology Laboratory, National Institute of Standards and Technology 105

Appendix II: Additional Material for the Record

Statement by Representative Eddie Bernice Johnson, Ranking Member, Committee on Science, Space, and Technology, U.S. House of Representatives 112

Letter submitted by Representative Barbara Comstock, Chairwoman, Subcommittee on Research, Committee on Science, Space, and Technology, U.S. House of Representatives 113

IS THE OPM DATA BREACH
THE TIP OF THE ICEBERG?

WEDNESDAY, JULY 8, 2015

House of Representatives,
Subcommittee on Research and Technology &
Subcommittee on Oversight,
Committee on Science, Space, and Technology,
Washington, D.C.

The Subcommittees met, pursuant to call, at 3:36 p.m., in Room 2318 of the Rayburn House Office Building, Hon. Barbara Comstock [Chairwoman of the Subcommittee on Research and Technology] presiding.

LAMAR S. SMITH, Texas
CHAIRMAN

EDDIE BERNICE JOHNSON, Texas
RANKING MEMBER

Congress of the United States
House of Representatives
COMMITTEE ON SCIENCE, SPACE, AND TECHNOLOGY

2321 RAYBURN HOUSE OFFICE BUILDING

WASHINGTON, DC 20515-6301

(202) 225-6371

www.science.house.gov

Subcommittees on Research and Technology and Oversight

Is the OPM Data Breach the Tip of the Iceberg?

Wednesday, July 8, 2015
2:00 p.m. to 4:00 p.m.
2318 Rayburn House Office Building

Witnesses

Mr. Michael R. Esser, *Assistant Inspector General for Audits, Office of Personnel Management*

Mr. David Snell, *Director, Federal Benefits Service Department, National Active and Retired Federal Employee Association*

Dr. Charles Romine, *Director, Information Technology Laboratory, National Institute of Standards and Technology*

Mr. Gregory Wilshusen, *Director, Information Security Issues, U.S. Government Accountability Office*

U.S. HOUSE OF REPRESENTATIVES
COMMITTEE ON SCIENCE, SPACE, AND TECHNOLOGY
SUBCOMMITTEES ON RESEARCH & TECHNOLOGY AND OVERSIGHT

Is the OPM Data Breach the Tip of the Iceberg?

Wednesday, July 8 2015
2:00 p.m. – 4:00 p.m.
2318 Rayburn House Office Building

Purpose

On Wednesday, July 8, 2015, the Research and Technology Subcommittee and Oversight Subcommittees will hold a joint hearing to examine recent data breaches at the Office of Personnel Management (OPM), discuss the implications of this breach for former and current employees as well as to the government, and identify the ongoing challenges for protecting personal and sensitive data government-wide from future cyber-attacks. The hearing will also review agency compliance with federal information security guidelines and standards required by the *Federal Information Security Management Act* (FISMA).[1] The Committee's jurisdiction includes the National Institute of Standards and Technology (NIST) who is responsible for key security standards and guidelines to support the implementation of and compliance with FISMA, the Department of Homeland Security's Science and Technology Directorate (DHS S&T) and research and development related to cybersecurity at the National Science Foundation (NSF).

Witnesses
- **Mr. Michael R. Esser,** Assistant Inspector General for Audits, Office of Personnel Management
- **Mr. David Snell**, Director, Federal Benefits Service Department, National Active and Retired Federal Employees Association
- **Dr. Charles Romine**, Director, Information Technology Laboratory, National Institute of Standards and Technology
- **Mr. Gregory Wilshusen**, Director, Information Security Issues, U.S. Government Accountability Office

Background

On June 4th, 2015 OPM announced that it had identified a cybersecurity breach affecting personnel data for approximately 4 million current and former federal employees, including personally identifiable information (PII).[2] As the investigation into the initial intrusion proceeded, the Interagency Response Team shared with relevant agencies that there was a high degree of confidence that OPM computer systems containing information on background investigations of current, former, and prospective Federal government employees, had been

---

[1] Federal Information Security Management Act of 2002 (Public Law 107-347), updated by the Federal Information Security Modernization Act of 2014 (Public Law 113-283).
[2] https://www.opm.gov/news/releases/2015/06/opm-to-notify-employees-of-cybersecurity-incident/

hacked. Early news reports, citing Federal Bureau of Investigation (FBI) sources, estimate that sensitive, personal information of 18 million people have been hacked by these computer breaches.[3] OPM is expected to provide an update on the extent of the second data breach this week.

OPM Investigation and Response

OPM discovered the first breach in April 2015, during the installation of new intrusion software. According to reports, in December 2014, intruders used a "zero-day" exploit — a previously unknown cyber-tool — to access information including "employees' Social Security numbers, job assignments, performance ratings and training information.[4] In testimony before the Senate Appropriations Financial Services and General Government Subcommittee, OPM Director Katherine Archuleta also testified that the intruders in the attack obtained a compromised user credential from a government contractor to help access the system.[5]

Since both incidents were discovered last April, OPM has partnered with the U.S. Department of Homeland Security's Computer Emergency Readiness Team (US-CERT), and the Federal Bureau of Investigation (FBI) to investigate and determine the full impact to federal personnel. Federal officials continue to investigate the source of the attack and assist with remediation efforts.[6] Although officials have not publicly identified the perpetrators, the Director of National Intelligence James Clapper called China a "leading suspect."[7]

OPM is in the process of sending notifications by mail and email to individuals whose information was compromised in the first breach. OPM signed a $21 million contract with the Winvale group and CSID to offer 18 months of credit monitoring and identity theft insurance.[8] Federal employees have since reported long wait times for assistance as well as "phishing campaigns masquerading as emails" from OPM and CSID.[9]

On June 29th, OPM announced the temporary suspension of the Electronic Questionnaires for Investigations Processing (E-QIP) system, a web-based platform used by federal employees to submit security background investigation forms with personal information, until more security measures are implemented.[10] OPM says that they are continuing to work with DHS and the FBI to determine the number of people affected by the second intrusion, and will begin making notifications to affected individuals in July.[11]

[3] http://www.cnn.com/2015/06/22/politics/opm-hack-18-milliion/index.html
[4] https://www.washingtonpost.com/world/national-security/chinese-hackers-breach-federal-governments-personnel-office/2015/06/04/889c0e52-0af7-11e5-95fd-d580f1c5d44e_story.html
[5] http://www.usatoday.com/story/news/politics/2015/06/27/opm-hack-questions-and-answers/29333211/
[6] http://www.opm.gov/news/latest-news/announcements/frequently-asked-questions/
[7] http://www.cnn.com/2015/06/25/politics/james-clapper-china-opm-hacking/
[8] http://www.washingtonpost.com/blogs/federal-eye/wp/2015/06/22/looking-for-help-after-the-federal-employee-hack-prepare-to-spend-a-few-hours-on-hold/
[9] http://www.nextgov.com/cybersecurity/2015/07/dhs-alerts-public-opm-related-phishing-scams/116794/
[10] https://www.opm.gov/news/releases/2015/06/opm-notifies-agencies-of-temporary-suspension-of-e-qip-system/
[11] http://www.washingtonpost.com/blogs/federal-eye/wp/2015/07/02/opm-plans-to-release-more-information-about-data-breach/

OPM Office of Inspector General (OIG) Audits

The OPM OIG has noted that "OPM has a history of struggling to comply with FISMA requirements." FISMA requires OIGs to perform annual audits of their agencies' IT security programs and practices. In 2007, the OPM OIG first identified an IT material weakness at OPM – a severe control deficiency that prohibits the organization from adequately protecting its data. Since that time the OPM OIG has continued to identify major security gaps in OPM's information systems. In 2014, the OPM OIG noted improvements, and changed the classification to a "significant deficiency, which is less serious than a material weakness." However the 2014 report continued to make 29 audit recommendations to OPM to improve technical security controls.[12]

History of Government Data Breaches

The number of cyber threats to both government and private sector information systems has grown exponentially in recent years. According to the U.S. Government Accountability Office (GAO), the number of information security incidents reported by federal agencies to US-CERT increased from 5,503 in fiscal year 2006 to 67,168 in fiscal year 2014 – an increase of over 1000 percent.[13] According to GAO, some recent examples of federal information system breaches include:

- In April 2015, the Department of Veterans Affairs (VA) Office of Inspector General reported that two VA contractors improperly accessed the VA network from foreign countries using personally owned equipment.
- In September 2014, a cyber-intrusion into the United States Postal Service's information systems may have compromised PII for more than 800,000 employees.
- In 2011, according to a media report, the Deputy Secretary of Defense acknowledged a significant cyber-attack in which a large number of files were taken by foreign intruders from a defense contractor. The deputy secretary was quoted as saying "it is a significant concern that over the past decade terabytes of data have been extracted by foreign intruders from corporate networks of defense companies" and that some of the data concerned "our most sensitive systems."[14]

In fiscal year 2014, the federal government spent more than $81 billion on information technology, and "Federal agencies spend a significant part of their annual IT funding on cybersecurity, which currently constitutes more than one in every eight dollars of agency IT budgets."[15]

---

[12] Statement of Michael R. Esser, Assistant Inspector General for Audits, Committee on Oversight and Government Reform, U.S. House of Representatives, June 16, 2015.

[13] *Actions Needed to Address Challenges Facing Federal Systems* GAO-15-573T, April 22, 2015 http://www.gao.gov/products/GAO-15-573T

[14] http://www.defense.gov/news/newsarticle.aspx?id=64686

[15] http://www.fas.org/sgp/crs/misc/R43831.pdf

A major consequence of a data breach is identity theft, whether the information is used to make purchases, obtain medical care or commit tax fraud. An estimated 12.7 million Americans experienced some sort of financial identity theft in 2014, costing $16 billion in financial losses. Many more Americans are at risk of identity theft, after numerous private and public sector breaches. The 2014 data breach of Anthem Health Insurance alone exposed the social security numbers of nearly 80 million Americans.[16] However, Cyber breaches to federal systems have wide-ranging consequences beyond identity theft, including the ability to adversely affect national security, damage public health and safety, and lead to inappropriate access to other sensitive personal information.

Federal Cybersecurity Laws and Regulations

The federal role in cybersecurity involves both security for federal systems and assisting in protecting nonfederal systems. More than 50 federal statutes address various aspects of cybersecurity.

The cybersecurity of federal systems is governed by FISMA, which was updated by the Federal Information Security Modernization Act (P.L. 113-283) in December 2014. FISMA created a security framework for federal information systems, with an emphasis on risk management, and gave specific responsibilities to the Office of Management and Budget (OMB), National Institutes of Standards and Technology (NIST), and the heads, chief information officers (CIOs), chief information security officers (CISOs), and inspectors general (IGs) of federal agencies.[17]

FISMA makes OMB responsible for overseeing federal information-security policy, evaluating agency programs, and promulgating cybersecurity standards developed by NIST. Each agency must designate an information-security officer, with responsibilities including agency-wide programs, policies, and procedures, training of security and other personnel, processes for remedial action to address deficiencies, and procedures for handling security incidents and ensuring continuity of operations. Agencies must also develop performance plans, conduct independent annual evaluations of their cybersecurity programs and practices, and provide annual reports on compliance and effectiveness to Congress. FISMA requirements also apply to contractors who run information systems on behalf of an agency.[18]

In December 2014, *The Cybersecurity Enhancement Act of 2015* (P.L. 113-270) passed the House and Senate and was signed into law. The new law strengthens the efforts of the National Science Foundation (NSF) and NIST in the areas of cybersecurity technical standards and cybersecurity awareness, education, and workforce development. P.L. 113-270 coordinates research and related activities conducted across the Federal agencies to better address evolving cyber threats.

---

[16] http://www.nbcnews.com/business/consumer/nearly-13-million-americans-victimized-id-thieves-2014-n316266
[17] *Information Security: Weaknesses Continue Amid New Federal Efforts to Implement Requirements*, GAO-12-137, October 2011, http://www.gao.gov/new.items/d12137.pdf
[18] *Cybersecurity: FISMA Reform*, CRS Insights, December 15, 2014.

Chairwoman COMSTOCK. The Subcommittees on Research and Technology and Oversight will come to order. Without objection, the Chair is authorized to declare recesses of the Subcommittees at any time.

Good afternoon. Our apologies for the delay. As you saw or heard, we were voting.

Welcome to today's hearing entitled ''Is the OPM Data Breach the Tip of the Iceberg?'' In front of you are packets containing the written testimony, biographies, and truth-in-testimony disclosures for today's witnesses.

I now recognize myself for five minutes for an opening statement.

Just over a month ago, the Office of Personnel Management (OPM) announced a massive data breach that exposed the personal information of over 4 million current and former federal employees and contractors. Like thousands of my fellow constituents and people across the country, I received a letter from OPM informing me that my personal information may have been compromised or stolen by criminals who are behind this attack.

Unfortunately, the news appears to be getting worse this week as we learn more about the reported second OPM data breach, compromising the security of potentially 18 million federal employees, contractors, and others who submitted sensitive information for background checks to the government. And sadly, the response from OPM has not inspired confidence over the past few weeks.

Identity theft by what seems to be a foreign entity is a very serious national security threat. They are literally, you know, at cyber war with us, and we as leaders have to appreciate that reality and operate in that reality.

Many of my constituents have contacted me about their fears and concerns. It has been months since OPM discovered the attack, and we still have too many questions and not enough answers. As we will hear from some of our witnesses today, federal employees have many unanswered questions. For example, just one: Are the credit monitoring identity theft provisions adequate? I know we've heard from people who are very concerned about whether they are.

Most alarming to me about these breaches is that they were launched less than 18 months after a previous severe network assault on OPM. We know that information security incidents reported by federal agencies has increased by 1,000 percent since 2006, 1,000 percent increase.

For years the OPM Office of Inspector General and the U.S. Government Accountability Office have been warning OPM leadership of critical vulnerabilities to their information systems. Some of the weakness and current problems were ID'd as far back as 2007. Today, many of their recommendations for fixing the systematic failures remain unmet.

Cyber criminals and foreign enemies are working night and day with the latest technology to exploit every vulnerability in our system, and it appears we're behind the times. The United States has some of the world's best technological minds and resources, yet our management in OPM does not appear to be getting up to speed.

Federal employees provide their sensitive personal information under the expectation that it is protected with all the seriousness that it should receive. However, that trust has now been broken and hence so many concerns.

Cybersecurity has to be a top priority in every government agency from the top Cabinet official on down. We need an aggressive, nimble, and flexible strategy to anticipate, intercept, and stop these cyber attacks. Those who are engaging in the attacks on our citizens, agencies, and companies, whether they be nation states, adversaries, or hacktivists and just, you know, random criminals are a reality that we'll be living with in the 21st century and we must develop and use all the tools and technology available to thwart them and understand this is going to be an ongoing problem that we have to constantly adapt to.

I want to note that we invited the OPM Chief Information Officer Donna Seymour to testify at today's hearing. She declined the Committee's invitation, citing other commitments, and we will continue to be working with them and asking them additional questions.

Today's panel of witnesses will help us better understand the magnitude of cybersecurity challenges at OPM across the federal government, as well as determine what steps need to be taken to prevent future cyber attacks and the state-of-the-art best practices to do so. And I should note that in the coming weeks we will also be looking at a lot of the best practices that the private sector has and other experts want to bring to bear that will probably reflect a lot of what you are going to be talking about today.

I appreciate the leadership of Chairman Lamar Smith on these issues and the role the Science Committee—that they have played in making cybersecurity research and development a priority.

I look forward to continuing to work on the Subcommittee on efforts to make sure the federal government is staying ahead of our adversaries. And if officials neglected their duties or are not the right people for the job, we also need to hold them accountable and make sure we are doing everything to improve the situation.

[The prepared statement of Chairwoman Comstock follows:]

PREPARED STATEMENT OF SUBCOMMITTEE ON RESEARCH & TECHNOLOGY
CHAIRWOMAN BARBARA COMSTOCK

Just over a month ago the Office of Personnel Management (OPM) announced a massive data breach that exposed the personal information of over 4 million current and former federal employees and contractors.

Like thousands of my fellow constituents, I received a letter from OPM informing me that my personal information may have been compromised or stolen by the criminals behind this attack.

Unfortunately, the news gets worse this week, as we learn more about the reported second OPM data breach, compromising the security of 18 million federal employees, contractors and others who submitted sensitive information for background checks. And sadly the response from OPM has not inspired confidence.

Identity theft by what seems to be a foreign entity is a very serious national security issue. They are at cyberwar with us—do our leaders appreciate that reality?

Many of my constituents have contacted me about their fears and concerns. It has been months since OPM discovered the attack, and we still have too many questions and not enough answers.

As we will hear from witnesses today, federal employees have many unanswered questions. Just one: Are the credit monitoring identity theft provisions adequate? Most alarming to me about these breaches is that they were launched less than 18 months after a previous severe network assault on OPM. We know that information security incidents reporting by federal agencies has increased by 1000 percent since 2006.

For years the OPM Office of Inspector General and the U.S. Government Accountability Office have been warning OPM leadership of critical vulnerabilities to their information systems. Some of the weakness and current problems were ID'd as far back as 2007. Today, many of their recommendations for fixing the systematic failures remain unmet.

Cyber criminals and foreign enemies are working night and day with the latest technology to exploit every vulnerability in our system, while OPM is behind the times and operating apparently at a pace with systems designed for the last century not for the current threat. The United States has some of the world's best technological minds and resources, yet OPM's management is failing.

Federal employees provide their sensitive personal information under the expectation that it is protected with all due seriousness. However, the trust between our federal employees, contractors, and others whose information has been compromised is damaged.

Cybersecurity must be a top priority in every government agency from the top Cabinet official on down. We need an aggressive, nimble, and flexible strategy to anticipate, intercept, and stop cyberattacks.

Those who are engaging in cyberattacks on our citizens, agencies, and companies—whether they be nation states, adversaries or hacktivists—are a reality we will be living with in the 21st century and we must develop and use all the tools and technology available to thwart them and understand this is an ongoing problem we have to constantly be on top of.

I want to note that we invited the OPM Chief Information Officer Donna Seymour to testify at today's hearing. She declined the Committee's invitation, citing other commitments, we continue to have questions about how and why this cyberattack occurred and the measures that have been instituted to prevent a future attack at OPM. We will take any necessary steps to ensure my constituents get those answers.

Today's panel of witnesses will help us better understand the magnitude of cybersecurity challenges at OPM and across the federal government, as well as determine what steps need to be taken to prevent future cyberattacks, and the state of the art best practices to do so.

I appreciate the leadership of Chairman Lamar Smith on these issues and the role the Science Committee has played in making cybersecurity R&D a priority.

I look forward to continuing to lead the Research & Technology Subcommittee in efforts to make sure the federal government is staying ahead of our adversaries who are constantly developing new and sophisticated malicious technologies.

If officials neglected their duties, or are not the right people for the job, they must be held accountable so that proper leadership is in place to not just meet, but anticipate and beat the next cyber threat.

Chairwoman COMSTOCK. So with that I will yield to the Ranking Member, but I also ask unanimous consent to place into the record various letters and articles that are relevant to the hearing.

[The information appears in Appendix II]

Chairwoman COMSTOCK. And without objection I'll now yield to the Ranking Member.

Mr. LIPINSKI. Thank you, Chairwoman Comstock. I want to thank you, Chairman Loudermilk, Chairman Smith, for holding this hearing on the recent OPM data breach. I want to thank all of our witnesses for being here this afternoon.

Unfortunately, major cyber attacks are happening more frequently. Today, we're going to talk about the significant breaches at the Office of Personnel Management. I have not received notification, but I believe I may have been a victim of this. But we all know that—I don't want to take away the significance of it but it's important to note there have been increasing number of cyber attacks in both the private and public sector where I know I've definitely been a victim of some of these attacks.

Several years ago, I began working on cybersecurity legislation, the Cybersecurity Enhancement Act, with my colleague Mr.

McCall. Our legislation dealt with cybersecurity standards, education, and workforce development. When we started, I said that I had no doubt that threats from individual hackers, criminal syndicates, and even other governments would grow and evolve along with our increased use of the internet. Unfortunately, I was right.

In February, Anthem, one of the Nation's largest health insurance companies, announced it suffered a cyber breach that compromised the records of 80 million current and former customers. And just last year, there were high-profile breaches at J.P. Morgan Chase, eBay, Target, and many others affecting millions of people.

Although I was happy that my bill with Mr. McCall was enacted at the end of last Congress, there is much, much more to do in the area of cybersecurity. Cybercrime and cyber espionage continue to threaten our national security, our critical infrastructure, businesses of all sizes, and every single American. This latest data breach at OPM is just another example of that.

In the OPM breach, millions of federal employees' personal information has been compromised, leading to significant concerns about how the stolen information will be used. Additionally, since OPM conducts more than 90 percent of all security clearance background investigations, this breach is an example of how cyber attacks threaten our national security. We must do better.

It'll take a collective effort in both the public and private sector to improve cybersecurity, and I cannot emphasize enough the importance of research into the social and behavioral aspects in this area. Our IT infrastructure is built, operated, and maintained by humans from the average worker at her desktop to Chief Information Officer of a major company or agency. Most cyber attacks are successful because of human error such as unwittingly opening a malicious email or allowing one's credentials to be compromised. Understanding the human element is necessary to combat threats and reduce risks.

To set governmentwide guidelines protecting federal information security systems, Congress passed—if I can turn my page—an example of human error here. Congress passed the Federal Information Security Modernization Act, or FISMA. FISMA, which was updated at the end of last Congress, requires federal agencies to develop, document, and implement an agencywide information security program.

Along with being responsible for their own information security system, the National Institute of Standards and Technology is tasked with developing standards and guidelines for all civilian federal information systems. Since NIST plays a critical role in protecting our nation's information security systems, it's important that they be part of this conversation. I'm happy that Dr. Romine is here today to tell us more about how NIST develops FISMA standards and how they work with other federal agencies.

FISMA also requires annual reviews of individual agencies' information security programs, as well as reviews of information security policies in the implementation of FISMA requirements governmentwide. I hope to hear from our witnesses about the steps necessary to ensure that OPM meets FISMA requirements, as well as how other agencies are doing in this space.

More information security systems, both in the public and private sector, will surely be subject to cyber attacks in the future, and while it's impossible to completely protect the connected information security system, we must do all we can to protect the personal information of millions of Americans and conduct the oversight to ensure such steps are taken. This hearing is the beginning of a conversation on how we can do that, and we must make sure that we follow through with action.

I look forward to our discussion this afternoon. Thank you, and I yield back the balance of my time.

[The prepared statement of Mr. Lipinski follows:]

PREPARED STATEMENT OF SUBCOMMITTEE
MINORITY RANKING MEMBER DANIEL LIPINSKI

Thank you Chairwoman Comstock and Chairman Loudermilk for holding this hearing on the recent OPM data breach. I want to thank all the witnesses for being here this afternoon.

Unfortunately, major cyber-attacks are happening more frequently. Today, we are going to talk about the significant breaches at the Office of Personnel Management (OPM). Not to take away from the significance of the OPM breach, I think it is important to note that there have been an increasing number of cyber-attacks in both the private and public sector.

Several years ago I began working on cybersecurity legislation, the Cybersecurity Enhancement Act, with my colleague, Mr. McCaul. Our legislation dealt with cybersecurity standards, education, and workforce development. When we started, I said that I had no doubt that threats from individual hackers, criminal syndicates, and even other governments would grow and evolve along with our increased use of the internet. Unfortunately, I was right.

In February, Anthem, one of the nation's largest health insurance companies, announced that it suffered a cyber-breach that compromised the records of 80 million current and former customers. And just last year there were high profile breaches at JP Morgan Chase, eBay, Target, and many others affecting millions of people.

Although I was happy that my bill with Mr. McCaul was enacted at the end of last Congress, there is much, much more to be done in the area of cybersecurity. Cybercrime and cyber-espionage continues to threaten our national security, our critical infrastructure, businesses of all sizes, and every single American. This latest data breach at OPM is just another example of that. In the OPM breach, millions of federal employees' personal information has been compromised, leading to significant concerns about how the stolen information will be used. Additionally, since OPM conducts more than 90 percent of all security clearance background investigations, this breach is an example of how cyber-attacks threaten our national security. We must do better.

It will take a collective effort of both the public and private sector to improve cybersecurity, and I cannot emphasize enough the importance of research into the social and behavioral aspects in this area. Our IT infrastructure is built, operated and maintained by humans, from the average worker at her desktop to the chief information officer of a major company or agency. Most cyber-attacks are successful because of human error, such as unwittingly opening a malicious email or allowing one's credentials to be compromised. Understanding the human element is necessary to combat threats and reduce risk.

To set government-wide guidelines for protecting federal information security systems, Congress passed the Federal Information Security Modernization Act or FISMA. FISMA, which was updated at the end of last Congress, requires federal agencies to develop, document, and implement an agency wide information security program.

Along with being responsible for their own information security system, the National Institute of Standards and Technology (NIST) is tasked with developing standards and guidelines for all civilian federal information systems. Since NIST plays a critical role in protecting our nation's information security systems, it is important that they be part of this conversation. I am happy that Dr. Romine is here today to tell us more about how NIST develops FISMA standards and how they work with other federal agencies.

FISMA also requires annual reviews of individual agencies' information security programs as well as reviews of information security policies and the implementation of FISMA requirements government-wide. I hope to hear from our witnesses about the steps necessary to ensure that OPM meets FISMA requirements, as well as how other agencies are doing in this space.

More information security systems—both in the public and private sector—will surely be subject to cyber-attacks in the future. And while it is impossible to completely protect a connected information security system, we must do all we can to protect the personal information of millions of Americans and conduct the oversight to ensure such steps are taken. This hearing is the beginning of a conversation on how we can do that and we must make sure that we follow through with action.

I look forward to our discussion this afternoon. Thank you and I yield back the balance of my time.

Chairwoman COMSTOCK. Thank you, Mr. Lipinski.

And I now recognize the Chair of the Oversight Subcommittee, the gentleman from Georgia, Mr. Loudermilk, for his opening statement.

Mr. LOUDERMILK. Thank you, Chairwoman Comstock, for holding this very important hearing on an issue that hits close to home for you, as many—as others in this country.

I'd like to thank our witnesses for being here today in order to help us understand what seems to be an epidemic of cyber attacks. I look forward to discussing what needs need to be done to prevent similar attacks from occurring in the future.

Now, it isn't a priority, nor it should be a priority for us just to address this because it affects some of us that are up here, but it's because it affects the American people. And unfortunately, this Administration has failed to provide Americans with any level of confidence that it will adequately protect their personal information when trusted with it.

As we have witnessed over the past few months, there has been a concerning pattern of security breaches involving government computer systems. This includes the recent, massive data breach of the Office of Personnel Management disclosing personal and official information that could potentially harm our national security. For an Administration that touts that it has ''prioritized the cybersecurity of federal departments and agencies,'' we have instead witnessed a government that is unable to properly secure its computer systems and protect sensitive information.

The situation at OPM is exactly why the subcommittee that I chair is looking into the collection of America's—Americans' personal data through the HealthCare.gov website. In that situation, it appears that Social Security numbers, dates of birth, names, mailing addresses, phone numbers, financial accounts information, military status, employment status, passport numbers, and taxpayer IDs are being retained. This information is being stored in a data warehouse that is intended to provide reporting and performance metrics related to the Federally Facilitated Marketplace and other HealthCare.gov-related systems.

In the situation of the data warehouse, the Administration never appeared to be forthright about the use and storage of personally identifiable information on HealthCare.gov. The Administration has yet to explain the reason for indefinitely storing user information, particularly of the users of the website who input their data to log in but do not end up enrolling.

While this Administration has claimed that cybersecurity is a priority, their actions on this and other issues regarding protecting the American people suggests the priorities are only lip service. From ending the Secure Cities program to storing critical information on American citizens without their approval or knowledge, this Administration is proving through their actions that protecting the American people is far from being on their list of priorities.

If that data warehouse is being protected in the same way that OPM was protecting personal information, action needs to be taken now to avoid putting the American people at significant personal risk. With many Americans being forced into the government healthcare exchange, a breach of this system could end up having millions affected, just like the OPM data hack.

The Government Accountability Office has included the cybersecurity of federal information systems on its list of high risk areas since 1997, so this isn't something new. Why, then, are we sitting here almost 20 years later, wondering why our federal information systems are not being adequately secured?

In the most recent GAO High Risk Series report, it says that ''Inspectors General at 22 of the 24 agencies cited information security as a major management challenge for their agency. For fiscal year 2014, most of the agencies had information security weaknesses in the majority of five key control categories.'' As Chairman of this subcommittee—this Committee's Oversight Subcommittee, I want to find the truth behind this reckless behavior that is threatening the safety and security of the American people. These actions—or rather, lack of actions—put the future of our nation at great risk and must stop.

I look forward to today's hearing, which I anticipate will inform us more about the recent OPM breach and the current state of our federal information systems. We owe it to the American people to ensure that their personally identifiable information is safe and protected from cybercriminals.

And with that, Madam Chair, I yield back.

[The prepared statement of Mr. Loudermilk follows:]

PREPARED STATEMENT OF OVERSIGHT SUBCOMMITTEE
CHAIRMAN BARRY LOUDERMILK

Thank you, Chairwoman Comstock, for holding this very important hearing on an issue that hits too close to home for you as well as many others in this country. I would like to thank our witnesses for being here today in order to help us understand what seems to be an epidemic of cyber-attacks. I look forward to discussing what needs to be done to prevent similar attacks from occurring in the future.

Unfortunately, this Administration has failed to provide Americans with any level of confidence that it will adequately protect their personal information when entrusted with it. As we have witnessed over the past few months, there has been a concerning pattern of security breaches involving government computer systems. This includes the recent, massive data breach of the Office of Personnel Management (OPM)—disclosing personal and official information that could potentially harm our national security. For an Administration that touts that it has ''prioritized the cybersecurity of federal departments and agencies,'' we have instead witnessed a government that is unable to properly secure its computer systems and protect sensitive information.

The situation at OPM is exactly why the Subcommittee that I Chair is looking into the collection of Americans' personal data through the HealthCare.gov website. In that situation, it appears that social security numbers, dates of birth, names, mailing addresses, phone numbers, financial accounts information, military status, employment status, passport numbers, and taxpayer IDs are being retained. This information is being stored in a "data warehouse that is intended to provide reporting and performance metrics related to the Federally Facilitated Marketplace (FFM) and other Healthcare.gov- related systems."

In the situation of the data warehouse, the Administration never appeared to be forthright about the use and storage of personally identifiable information on HealthCare.gov. The Administration has yet to explain the reason for indefinitely storing user information, particularly of the users of the website who input their data to log in, but do not end up enrolling.

If that data warehouse is being protected in the same way that OPM was protecting personal information, action needs to be taken now to avoid putting the American people at significant personal risk. With many Americans being forced into the government health care exchange, a breach of this system could end up having millions affected, just like the OPM data hack.

The Government Accountability Office (GAO) has included the cybersecurity of federal information systems on its list of high risk areas since 1997, so this isn't something new. Why, then, are we sitting here almost twenty years later, wondering why our federal information systems are not being adequately secured? In the most recent GAO High Risk Series report, it says that "... inspectors general at 22 of the 24 agencies cited information security as a major management challenge for their agency. For fiscal year 2014, most of the agencies had information security weaknesses in the majority of five key control categories."

As the Chairman of this Committee's Oversight Subcommittee, I want to find the truth behind this reckless behavior that is threatening the safety and security of the American people. These actions—or rather, lack of actions—put the future of our nation at great risk, and must stop.

I look forward to today's hearing, which I anticipate will inform us more about the recent OPM breach and the current state of our federal information systems. We owe it to the American people to ensure that their personally identifiable information is safe and protected from cybercriminals.

Chairwoman COMSTOCK. Thank you, Chairman Loudermilk.

And I now recognize the Ranking Member of the Subcommittee on Oversight, the gentleman from Virginia, my colleague Mr. Beyer, for his opening statement.

Mr. BEYER. Thank you, Madam Chair. And thank you, Chairs Comstock and Loudermilk, for holding this hearing today, incredibly timely and—because, you know, earlier today obviously New York Stock Exchange, United Airlines, the Wall Street Journal all suffering from computer glitches that has disrupted their computer networks. And whether this turns out to be intentional or whether—or not, it certainly highlights the potential vulnerabilities of our digital dependence. And today's hearing obviously is about Office of Personnel Management.

Deterring, detecting, and defending against the multitude of online threats that constantly lurk in the cyberspace domain is a critical issue for federal agencies and the federal government and the private sector alike. Last year alone, federal agencies reported nearly 70,000 individual computer security incidents to the U.S. Computer Emergency Readiness Team, or CERT. During the same time period, October 1, 2013, to September 30, 2014, nonfederal entities reported more than 570,000 incidents and many other incidents are potentially not identified or even not reported at all. Cyber threats are constant, they're evolving, they're very sophisticated, and many pose serious distress to companies, agencies, and individuals.

The two recent data breaches at OPM are particularly important to me and to my constituents. Representing a Congressional District just outside the Nation's capital, many of my constituents are federal employees who may have had their personal data compromised as a result of these intrusions. One of those attacks is believed to have compromised the personal information of more than four million people and the other, up to 14 million people. And I'm particularly troubled that the data that was reportedly accessed included not just the personnel files but the security files of our defense, homeland security, and intelligence community employees. This could potentially jeopardize the financial security, personal safety, and ultimately the secrets that are entrusted to help protect the Nation.

While the facts of this case are still being unraveled, including the motive for the attack, the identity of the perpetrators and the potential damage they may have caused, we should understand, too, that the federal government is not alone in being the victim of cyber attacks. In the past year hundreds of millions of personal records have been compromised by hackers targeting J.P. Morgan Chase, eBay, Home Depot, Target, and other private companies. I seem to receive a new credit card or debit card about every 6 weeks from my bank with a note telling me that the card has been compromised yet again.

When I was in Switzerland, a State Department computer was hacked in one year, the Defense Department the next. The newspapers blamed China and Russia. Still, the OPM was significant and I'm particularly impacted—concerned about the impact this has on the morale of a federal workforce that recently has endured, through no fault of their own, a government shutdown, forced furloughs, staffing cuts, pay freezes. These government employees now have the added insult of a breach of their personal data.

Agency heads should also be mindful and accommodating of the impact of federal employees who need time off to mitigate the fallout from this hack. And I encourage OPM to communicate with all agencies to ensure that workers are accommodated so they can visit their banks, Social Security offices, creditors in order to deal with the repercussions of the breach.

I know every time I get a new card, I get four or five people that don't get paid because the card numbers change and then they call and—I know it upsets my wife terribly.

I'm also concerned that the reports of this attack suggest it may have been the result of individuals with ties to foreign entities and that particularly a private company working for the government as a security contractor may have been the weak link in the chain of events that led to the successful attack.

We're making steady, slow progress in fortifying our cyber defenses from potential attack. According to OMB's annual report on FISMA sent to Congress in February, there's been monitoring—improvement in federal agencies implementing continuous monitoring of their networks and the authentication of their users, for instance, but these results are not good enough. I know everyone on the panel here is interested in learning what we can do to strengthen the system as quickly as possible, as strongly as possible, recognizing that we're never going to have 100 percent security, that the creative hackers, ever younger, will figure out additional ways around it. How can we create the very best advice on closing cybersecurity holes if and when they exist and then augmenting our security defenses against them?

So I very much look forward to your testimony and your advice, and Madam Chair, I yield back.

[The prepared statement of Mr. Beyer follows:]

PREPARED STATEMENT OF SUBCOMMITTEE ON OVERSIGHT
MINORITY RANKING MEMBER DONALD S. BEYER, JR.

Thank you Chairs Comstock and Loudermilk for holding this hearing today. I believe this is an important hearing and I look forward to hearing from our witnesses. I believe this is an important and timely hearing. Earlier today it was reported that the New York Stock Exchange, United Airlines and Wall Street Journal are all suffering from a "computer glitch" that has disrupted their computer networks. Whether this event is determined to be intentional or not it highlights the potential vulnerability of our digital dependence. Today's hearing, however, is about another computer incident at the Office of Personnel Management or OPM.

Deterring, detecting and defending against the multitude of on-line threats that constantly lurk in the cyberspace domain is a critical issue for the federal government and private sector alike.Last year alone federal agencies reported nearly 70,000 individual computer security incidents to the U.S. Computer Emergency Readiness Team or CERT. During the same time period, from October 1, 2013 to September 30, 2014, non-Federal entities reported more than 570,000 incidents and many other incidents are potentially not identified and others not reported at all.

Cyber threats are constant and evolving, some are very sophisticated and many pose serious distress to companies, agencies and individuals. The two recent data breaches of the Office of Personnel Management (OPM) are particularly important to me and my constituents.Representing a congressional district just outside the nation's Capital many of my constituents are federal employees who may have had their personal data compromised as a result of these intrusions. One of those attacks is believed to have compromised the personal information of more than 4 million individuals and the other is suspected to have compromised the data of as many as 14 million people. I am particularly troubled that the data that was reportedly accessed included not just the personnel files but the security files of our defense, homeland security and intelligence community employees. This could potentially jeopardize their financial security, personal safety and ultimately the secrets they are entrusted to help protect for our Nation.

While the facts of this case are still being unraveled, including the motive for the attack, the identities of the perpetrators and the potential damage they may have caused, we should understand too that the federal government is not alone in being victim to cyberattacks. In the past year, hundreds of millions of personal records have been compromised by hackers targeting JP Morgan Chase, Ebay, Home Depot and other private companies.

Still, the OPM breach was significant. I am concerned for the personal and professional impact of this breach on our dedicated federal workforce, particularly those involved in the national security arena. It should not be understated the impact this has on the morale of a workforce that has recently endured—through no fault of their own—a government shutdown, forced furloughs, staffing cuts, and pay freezes. These government employees now have the added insult of a breach of their personal data.

Agency heads should also be mindful and accommodating of impacted federal employees who need time off to mitigate the fallout from the hack. I encourage OPM to communicate with all agencies to ensure workers are accommodated so that they can visit their banks, Social Security offices, and creditors in order to deal with the repercussions of the breach.

I am also concerned that reports of this attack suggest it may have been the result of individuals with ties to foreign entities and I am concerned that it appears a private company working for the government as a security contractor may have been the weak link in the chain of events that ultimately led to a successful attack.

The federal government is making steady, but slow progress in fortifying our cyber defenses from potential attack. According to the Office of Management and Budget's (OMB's) annual report on the Federal Information Security Management Act (FISMA) sent to Congress in February there has been improvement in federal agencies implementing continuous monitoring of their networks and the authentication of their users, for instance. But the results are still not good enough. Federal Agencies need to do a better job meeting the IT security criteria demanded by compliance with FISMA and they need to apply the cyber security standards recommended by the National Institute of Standards and Technology (NIST) to their networks. At the same time, Congress and the public need to realize that no matter how well protected an Agency or private entity is that they will never be 100-percent secure and that data breaches are bound to occur in the future.

I hope our witnesses can help provide us with advice on closing cyber-security holes when and where they exist and augmenting our security defenses against them.

With that I yield back.

Chairwoman COMSTOCK. Thank you, Mr. Beyer. And thank you for your leadership on this, too, and being upfront on it.

I now recognize the Chairman of the full committee, Mr. Smith.

Chairman SMITH. Thank you, Madam Chair.

Today's hearing highlights the latest and, so far, the most extensive cybersecurity failure by a federal agency, the theft of millions of federal employee records from the Office of Personnel Management.

National defense in our digital age no longer just means protecting ourselves against enemies who attack with traditional weapons. It now means protecting America from those who launch cyber attacks against our computers and networks, invading our privacy and probably endangering lives.

But it is about much more than solely the invasion of privacy or the burden to our economy. This is a national security concern, as these breaches expose information about members of our military and employees of national security agencies.

A number of federal agencies guard America's cybersecurity interests. Several are under the jurisdiction of the Science Committee. These include the National Science Foundation, the National Institute of Standards and Technology, the Department of Homeland Security's Science and Technology Directorate, and the Department of Energy. All of these agencies support critical research and development to promote cybersecurity and set federal standards. However, it is clear that too many federal agencies like OPM fail to meet the basic standards of information security, and no one is being held accountable.

Last year audits revealed that 19 of 24 major federal agencies failed to meet the basic cybersecurity standards mandated by law. And yet the Administration has allowed deficient systems to stay online. What are the consequences when a federal agency fails to meet its basic duties to protect sensitive information? So far it seems the only people penalized are the millions of innocent Americans who have had their personal information exposed. It will be some time before we know the full extent of the damage to personal and national security caused by the OPM breach of security. But we do know that it is critical that we prevent further attacks on America's cyber systems.

The federal government failed in its responsibility to keep sensitive and personal information secure, and Americans deserve better. The Science Committee will continue its efforts to support the research and development essential to strengthen our Nation's cyber defenses. We will also continue to demand better answers from OPM on the extent of this breach.

The Director of the Office of Personnel Management recently testified: ''I don't believe anyone (at OPM) is personally responsible.'' That is not believable. In fact, it's an insult to the American people who pay her salary. The government should be accountable to the people, and this committee will continue to demand answers about who is responsible for failing to keep Americans' sensitive information secure. I hope we can use lessons learned from the OPM breach to help find solutions to prevent the next attack.

I look forward to hearing from our witnesses today and I'll yield back.

[The prepared statement of Chairman Smith follows:]

PREPARED STATEMENT OF COMMITTEE CHAIRMAN LAMAR S. SMITH

Thank you Madam Chair. Today's hearing highlights the latest and so far the most extensive cybersecurity failure by a federal agency - the theft of millions of federal employee records from the Office of Personnel Management (OPM).

National defense in the digital age no longer just means protecting ourselves against enemies who attack with traditional weapons. It now means protecting America from those who launch cyber-attacks against our computers and networks, invading our privacy and probably endangering lives.

But it is about much more than solely the invasion of privacy or the burden to our economy. This is a national security concern as these breaches expose information about members of our military and employees of national security agencies.

A number of federal agencies guard America's cybersecurity interests. Several are under the jurisdiction of the Science Committee. These include the National Science Foundation, the National Institute of Standards and Technology, the Department of Homeland Security's Science and Technology Directorate, and the Department of Energy.

All of these agencies support critical research and development to promote cybersecurity and set federal standards. However it is clear that too many federal agencies like OPM fail to meet the basic standards of information security—and no one is being held accountable.

Last year audits revealed that 19 of 24 major federal agencies failed to meet the basic cybersecurity standards mandated by law. And yet the Administration has allowed deficient systems to stay online.

What are the consequences when a federal agency fails to meet its basic duties to protect sensitive information? So far it seems the only people penalized are the millions of innocent Americans who have had their personal information exposed.

It will be some time before we know the full extent of the damage to personal and national security caused by the OPM breach of security. But we do know that it is critical that we prevent further attacks on America's cyber systems.

The federal government failed in its responsibility to keep sensitive and personal information secure, and Americans deserve better.

The Science Committee will continue its efforts to support the research and development essential to strengthen our Nation's cyber defenses. We will also continue to demand better answers from OPM on the extent of this breach.

The Director of the Office of Personnel Management recently testified: "I don't believe anyone (at OPM) is personally responsible." That is not believable. In fact, it's an insult the American people who pay her salary.

The government should be accountable to the people, and this Committee will continue to demand answers about who is responsible for failing to keep Americans' sensitive information secure.

I hope we can use lessons learned from the OPM breach to help find solutions to prevent the next attack. I look forward to hearing from our witnesses today and yield back.

Chairwoman COMSTOCK. Thank you, Mr. Chairman.

And if there are Members who wish to submit additional opening statements, your statements will be added to the record at this point.

Now at this time I would like to introduce our witnesses. Michael Esser is the Assistant Inspector General for Audits at the Office of Personnel Management. In this role, Mr. Esser is responsible for overseeing audits of OPM's information systems. Prior to joining the office in 1991 he worked in northern Virginia as a CPA. Mr. Esser holds a bachelor of science degree in accounting and a master's degree in business administration from George Mason University.

Our second witness today is David Snell, Director of the Federal Benefits Service Department for the National active and Retired Federal Employees Association, which represents some 300,000 active and retired federal employees and their spouses. Before joining there, Mr. Snell worked for nearly three decades at OPM ending his career there as Chief of Retirement Benefits Branch. He holds a bachelor of science degree from George Mason University. We have a theme here. Great university.

Our third witness today is Dr. Charles Romine, Director of the Information Technology Laboratory at the National Institute of Standards and Technology. This program develops and disseminates standards for security and reliability of information systems, including cybersecurity standards and guidelines for federal agencies like OPM. Dr. Romine has previously served as a Senior Policy Analyst at the White House Office of Science and Technology Policy and as a Program Manager at the Department of Energy's Advanced Scientific Computing Research Office. Dr. Romine received his bachelor's degree in mathematics and his Ph.D. in applied mathematics from the University of Virginia.

Today's final witness is Dr. Gregory—let me get this right—Wilshusen. Okay. Mr. Wilshusen is the Director of Information Security Issues at the U.S. Government Accountability Office. Prior to joining GAO in 1997, Mr. Wilshusen was a Senior Systems Analyst at the Department of Education. He received his bachelor's degree in business administration from the University of Missouri—I guess the non-Virginia university here—and his master of science in information management from George Washington University, close enough.

In order to allow time for discussion, please limit your testimony to five minutes. Your entire written statement will be made part of the record.

I now recognize Mr. Esser for five minutes to present his testimony.

TESTIMONY OF MR. MICHAEL R. ESSER, ASSISTANT INSPECTOR GENERAL FOR AUDITS, OFFICE OF PERSONNEL MANAGEMENT

Mr. ESSER. Chairwoman, Chairman, Ranking Members, and Members of the Committee, good afternoon. My name is Michael Esser and I am the Assistant Inspector General for audits at the U.S. Office of Personnel Management. Thank you for inviting me to testify at today's hearing on the IT security work done by my office at OPM.

OPM has a long history of systemic failures to properly manage its IT infrastructure, which may have ultimately led to the recent data breaches. We are pleased to see that the agency is taking steps to improve its IT security posture but many challenges still lay ahead.

To begin, I would like to discuss some of the findings from our annual audits under the Federal Information Security Management Act, known as FISMA. We have identified three general areas of concern which are discussed in detail in my written testimony.

The first area is information security governance. This is the management structure and processes that form the foundation of a successful security program. It is vital to have a centralized governance structure. OPM has made improvements in this area but it is still working to recover from years of decentralization.

The second area is security assessments and authorizations. This is a comprehensive assessment of each IT system to ensure that it meets the applicable security standards before allowing the system to operate. Our 2014 FISMA audit found that 11 of OPM's 47 major systems were operating without a valid authorization. Because of actions taken by the CIO in April 2015 we expect this number to more than double by the end of fiscal year 2016.

The third area is technical security controls. OPM has implemented a variety of controls to make the agency's IT systems more secure. However, these tools must be used properly and must cover the entire IT environment. Our FISMA audit last year found that they were not.

These areas represent fundamental weaknesses in OPM's IT security program that have been reported to the OPM Director, OMB, and the Congress for many years. The fact that these longstanding issues were allowed to continue for so long without being taken seriously raises questions about the inherent effectiveness of the original FISMA legislation and implementing guidelines.

Since 2002 the IGs have been reviewing their agencies' information security programs, but the reporting guidelines from OMB were focused on compliance with specific security areas and lacked perspective on the overall effectiveness of the agency's program.

The FISMA Modernization Act of 2014 shifts the focus from review and compliance to assessing effectiveness of security controls. In addition, a new maturity model approach to evaluating the state of agencies' continuous monitoring programs was introduced in this year's FISMA reporting instructions for OIGs. These new developments should go a long way toward improving the IT security programs of federal agencies. OMB and DHS should also work toward making the OIG FISMA reporting metrics more reflective of the current risks and threats and further adopting the maturity model approach for other reporting domains.

I would also like to take a moment to discuss e-QIP, the IT system that OPM uses to collect information related to federal background investigations. Just last week, OPM disabled the system due to serious vulnerabilities detected in the design of the database and public facing website. While we agree with the actions taken, OPM has known about vulnerabilities in the system for years but has not corrected them. During the 2012 security assessment and authorization process for e-QIP, an independent assessor identified 18 security vulnerabilities which still remain open and unaddressed today. We believe this is an example of the importance of the security assessment process and also of OPM's historical negligence of IT security in general.

Moving forward, OPM is undertaking a massive infrastructure improvement project which, when completed, should significantly improve the agency's IT security posture. However, we identified several concerns related to OPM's failure to follow proper project management processes and the agency's use of a sole-source contract. These are discussed in more detail in my written testimony.

We fully support OPM's modernization efforts but we are concerned that if this project is not done correctly, the agency will be in a worse situation than it is today and millions of taxpayer dollars will have been wasted.

Thank you for your time and I'm happy to answer any questions.

[The prepared statement of Mr. Esser follows:]

Office of the Inspector General
United States Office of Personnel Management

Statement of
Michael R. Esser
Assistant Inspector General for Audits

before the

Subcommittee on Research and Technology

and the

Subcommittee on Oversight

Committee on Science, Space, and Technology

United States House of Representatives

on

"Is the OPM Data Breach the Tip of the Iceberg?"

July 8, 2015

Chairwoman Comstock, Chairman Loudermilk, Ranking Member Lipinski, Ranking Member Beyer, and Members of the Subcommittees:

Good morning. My name is Michael R. Esser. I am the Assistant Inspector General for Audits at the U.S. Office of Personnel Management (OPM). Thank you for inviting me to testify at today's hearing to discuss our office's information technology (IT) security audit work, including our oversight of OPM's response to the recent data breaches and our annual audits required by the Federal Information Security Management Act, commonly known as "FISMA." Although OPM has made progress in certain areas, some of the current problems and weaknesses were identified as far back as Fiscal Year (FY) 2007. We believe this long history of systemic failures to properly manage its IT infrastructure may have ultimately led to the security breaches and loss of sensitive personal data at OPM.

OIG's FISMA Work

FISMA requires that Offices of Inspector General (OIGs) perform annual audits of their agencies' IT security programs and practices. These audits are conducted in accordance with guidance issued each year by the U.S. Department of Homeland Security (DHS) Office of Cybersecurity and Communications.

Today I will talk about three of the most significant concerns highlighted in our FY 2014 FISMA report. However, it is important to note that our report contained a total of 29 recommendations covering a wide variety of IT security topics. Only 3 of these 29 recommendations have been closed to date, and 9 of the open recommendations are long-standing issues that were rolled-forward from prior year FISMA audits.

1. Information Security Governance

Information security governance is the management structure and processes that form the foundation of a successful IT security program. Although the DHS FISMA reporting metrics do not directly address security governance, it is an overarching issue that impacts how the agency handles IT security and its ability to meet FISMA requirements, and therefore we have always addressed the matter in our annual FISMA audit reports.

This is an area where OPM has seen significant improvement. However, some of the past weaknesses still haunt the agency today.

In the FY 2007 FISMA report, we identified a material weakness[1] related to the lack of IT security policies and procedures. In FY 2009, we expanded the material weakness to include the lack of a centralized security management structure necessary to implement and enforce IT security policies. OPM's Office of the Chief Information Officer (OCIO) was responsible for the agency's overall technical infrastructure and provided boundary-level security controls for the systems residing on this infrastructure. However, each OPM program office had primary responsibility for managing security controls specific to its own IT systems. There was often confusion and disagreement as to which controls were the responsibility of the OCIO, and which were the responsibility of the program offices.

Further, the program office personnel responsible for IT security frequently had no IT security background and were performing this function in addition to another full-time role. For example, this meant that an employee whose job was processing retirement applications may have been given the additional responsibility of monitoring and managing the IT security needs of the system used to process those applications.

---

[1] An IT material weakness is a severe control deficiency that prohibits the organization from adequately protecting its data.

As a result of this decentralized governance structure, many security controls went unimplemented and/or remained untested, and OPM routinely failed a variety of FISMA metrics year after year. Therefore, we continued to identify this security governance issue as a material weakness in all subsequent FISMA audits through FY 2013.

However, in FY 2014, we changed the classification of this issue to a significant deficiency, which is less serious than a material weakness. This change was prompted by important improvements that were the result of changes instituted in recent years by OPM. Specifically, in FY 2012, the then OPM Director issued a memorandum mandating the centralization of IT security duties to a team of Information System Security Officers (ISSO) that report to the OCIO. In FY 2014, the OPM Director approved a plan to further restructure the OCIO that included funding for additional ISSO positions. The OCIO also established a 24/7 security operations center responsible for monitoring IT security events for the entire agency; however, OPM's continuous monitoring program cannot yet be classified as "mature" because the agency continues to rely on periodic ad hoc testing of security controls.

This new governance structure has resulted in improvement in the consistency and quality of security practices for the various IT systems owned by the agency. Although we are optimistic that these improvements will continue, it is apparent that the OCIO continues to be negatively impacted by years of decentralized security governance, as the technical infrastructure remains fragmented and therefore inherently difficult to protect.

2. Security Assessment and Authorization

A Security Assessment and Authorization (Authorization) is a comprehensive process under which the IT security controls of an information system are thoroughly assessed against applicable security standards. After the assessment is complete, a formal "Authorization to Operate" (ATO) memorandum is signed, indicating that the system is cleared to operate in the agency's technical environment. The Office of Management and Budget (OMB) mandates that all major Federal information systems be re-authorized every three years unless a mature continuous monitoring system is in place (which OPM does not yet have). Although, as mentioned, IT security responsibility is being centralized under the OCIO, it is still the responsibility of OPM program offices to facilitate and pay for the Authorization process for the IT systems that they own.

There has been some discussion over the past few weeks regarding the importance of Authorizations. It is true that the ATO itself is simply a piece of paper and does not, in itself, indicate that a system is secure. Conversely, the lack of an ATO does not necessarily mean that a system is *not* secure. However, it is important to note that the intent of the ATO is to certify that a system was subject to the entire Authorization *process*. An agency IT system must be subjected to a thorough and independent assessment in order to determine whether the necessary security controls are in place and functioning appropriately. Without such an assessment, the agency will not know what weaknesses and vulnerabilities may be present. If the agency does not know what weaknesses and vulnerabilities exist in its IT environment, it cannot take steps to address and remove those weaknesses, or develop a proactive and comprehensive IT security strategy.

OPM has a long history of issues related to system Authorizations, which we believe represents a long-standing pattern of neglect of IT security. Our FY 2010 FISMA audit report contained a material weakness related to incomplete, inconsistent, and poor quality Authorization packages. This issue improved over the next two years, and was removed as an audit concern in FY 2012.

However, problems with OPM's system Authorizations have recently resurfaced. In FY 2014, 21 OPM systems were due for Authorization, but 11 of those were not completed on time and were therefore operating without a valid Authorization.[2] This is a drastic increase from prior years, and represents a systemic issue of inadequate planning by OPM program offices to assess and authorize the information systems that they own.

Although the majority of our FISMA audit work is performed towards the end of the fiscal year, it already appears that there will be a greater number of systems this year operating without a valid Authorization. In April, the CIO issued a memorandum that granted an extension of the previous Authorizations for all systems whose Authorization had already expired, and for those scheduled to expire through September 2016. Should this moratorium on Authorizations continue, the agency will have up to 23 systems that have not been subject to a thorough security controls assessment. The justification for this action was that OPM is in the process of modernizing its IT infrastructure and once this modernization is complete, all systems would have to receive new Authorizations anyway.

While we support the OCIO's effort to modernize its systems, this action to extend Authorizations is contrary to OMB guidance, which specifically states that an "extended" or "interim" Authorization *is not valid*. Consequently, these systems are still operating without a current Authorization, as they have not been subject to the complete security assessment process that the ATO is intended to represent. We believe that this continuing disregard of the importance of the Authorization process is an indication that the agency has not historically, and still does not, prioritize IT security.

There are currently no consequences for failure to meet FISMA standards, or operate systems without Authorizations, at either the agency level or the program office level. The OIG simply reports our findings in our annual FISMA audit, which is delivered to OPM and then posted on our website. OMB receives the results of all FISMA audits, and produces an annual report to Congress. There are no directives or laws that provide for penalties for agencies that fail to meet FISMA requirements.

However, at the program office level, OPM has the authority to institute administrative sanctions. This could be an effective way to reduce non-compliance with FISMA requirements. In addition, we recommended that the employee performance standards of all OPM major system

---

[2] The OIG is the co-owner of one of these IT systems, the Audit Reports and Receivables Tracking System. This system has been reclassified as a minor system on the OPM general support system (GSS), and cannot be Authorized until the OCIO Authorizes the GSS.

owners include a requirement related to FISMA compliance for the systems they own and it be included as part of their annual performance evaluation as a critical element. Since OMB requires a valid Authorization for all Federal IT systems, we also recommended that the OPM Director *consider* shutting down systems that were in violation. Again, we acknowledge that the lack of an ATO does not, by definition, mean that a system is insecure. However, it absolutely does mean that a system is at a significantly higher risk of containing security vulnerabilities. The authorization process – nearly without exception – identifies significant issues that must be addressed. Considering the rapidly changing pace of technology, it is irresponsible to allow these systems to operate indefinitely without routinely subjecting them to a thorough security controls assessment.

Not only was a large volume (11 out of 47 systems) of OPM's IT systems operating without a valid Authorization, but several of these systems are among the most critical and sensitive applications owned by the agency.

Two of the OCIO systems without an Authorization are general support systems that host a variety of other major applications. Over 65 percent of all systems operated by OPM (not including contractor-operated systems) reside on one of these two support systems, and are therefore subject to any security risks that exist on the support systems.

Furthermore, two additional systems without Authorizations are owned by OPM's Federal Investigative Services, which is responsible for facilitating background investigations for suitability and security clearance determinations. Any weaknesses in the IT systems supporting this program office could potentially have national security implications.

As I explained, maintaining active Authorizations for all IT systems is a critical element of a Federal information security program, and failure to thoroughly assess and address a system's security weaknesses increases the risk of a security breach. We believe that the volume and sensitivity of OPM systems that are operating without an active Authorization represents a material weakness in the internal control structure of the agency's IT security program.

3. Technical Security Controls

As previously stated, our FY 2014 FISMA report contained a total of 29 audit recommendations, but two of the most critical areas in which OPM needs to improve its technical security controls relate to configuration management and authentication to IT systems using personal identity verification (PIV) credentials.

Configuration management refers to the policies, procedures, and technical controls used to ensure that IT systems are securely deployed. OPM has implemented a variety of new controls and tools designed to strengthen the agency's technical infrastructure by ensuring that its network devices are configured securely. However, our FY 2014 FISMA audit determined that all of these tools are not being utilized to their fullest capacity. For example, we were told in an interview with OPM personnel that OPM performs monthly vulnerability scans on all computer servers using its automated scanning tools. While we confirmed that OPM does indeed own these tools and that regular scan activity was occurring, our audit also determined that some of the scans were not working correctly because the tools did not have the proper credentials, and that some servers were not scanned at all.

OPM has also implemented a comprehensive security information and event management tool designed to automatically correlate potential security incidents by analyzing a variety of devices simultaneously. However, at the time of our FY 2014 FISMA report, this tool was receiving data from only 80 percent of OPM's major IT systems.

During this audit we also determined that OPM does not maintain an accurate centralized inventory of all servers and databases that reside within the network. Even if the tools I just referenced were being used appropriately, OPM cannot fully defend its network without a comprehensive list of assets that need to be protected and monitored.

This issue ties back to the centralized governance issue I discussed earlier. Each OPM program office historically managed its own inventory of devices supporting their respective information systems. Even though the OCIO is now responsible for all of OPM's IT systems, it still has significant work ahead in identifying all of the assets and data that it is tasked with protecting.

With respect to PIV authentication, OMB required all Federal IT systems to be upgraded to use PIV for multi-factor authentication by the beginning of FY 2012. OMB guidance also mandates that all new systems under development must be PIV-compliant prior to being made operational.

In FY 2012, the OCIO began an initiative to require PIV authentication to access the agency's network. As of the end of FY 2014, over 95 percent of OPM workstations required PIV authentication to access the OPM network. However, none of the agency's 47 major applications required PIV authentication. Full implementation of PIV authentication would go a long way in protecting an agency from security breaches, as an attacker would need to compromise more than a username and password to gain unauthorized access to a system. Consequently, we believe that PIV authentication for all systems should be a top priority for OPM.

Some of the other areas where we identified technical control weaknesses include:

- Baseline configurations: OPM has not documented pre-approved secure configurations for the operating systems it utilizes;

- Configuration change control: OPM cannot ensure that all changes made to information systems have been properly documented and approved;

- Patch management: Our vulnerability scan test work determined that numerous servers were not patched on a timely basis; and,

- VPN connections: VPN connections do not time out after 30 minutes of inactivity.

Modernizing OPM's IT Environment

OPM, like other Federal agencies, is facing the daunting, but not impossible, challenge of modernizing its IT environment.

In the past few weeks, there have been assertions that OPM's legacy information systems are supported by very old technology (specifically COBOL, a mainframe programming language), and therefore could not be protected by modern security controls. However, we know from our audit work that some of the OPM systems involved in the data breaches run on modern operating and database management systems. Consequently, modern security technology such as encryption or data loss prevention could have been implemented on these specific systems.

Also, OPM has stated that because the agency's IT environment is based on legacy technology, it is necessary to complete a full overhaul of the existing technical infrastructure in order to address the immediate security concerns. While we agree in principle that this is an ideal future goal for the agency's IT environment, there are steps that OPM can take (or has already taken) to secure its current IT environment.

For example, OPM has significantly upgraded security controls to protect the perimeter of its network. In addition, some of OPM's most sensitive systems are compatible with additional security controls such as data encryption and other data loss prevention techniques, which could be utilized to protect OPM's systems. Another step that OPM could take would be implementing full two-factor authentication to access OPM's major IT systems. This would add an additional layer of defense that will go a long way toward preventing additional data breaches.

A more in-depth process for improving the security of OPM's systems will involve a comprehensive analysis of their fundamental design. OPM recently disabled access to its Electronic Questionnaire for Investigations Processing system (referred to as e-QIP), which is used to collect information related to Federal background investigations, because of serious vulnerabilities detected in the design of the database and public-facing website.

OPM's official statement on this issue claims that the agency is acting proactively by shutting down the e-QIP system. However, the current security review ordered for this system is a direct reaction to the recent security breaches. In fact, the e-QIP system contains vulnerabilities that OPM knew about, but had failed to correct for years. As part of the system's Authorization process in September 2012, an independent assessor identified 18 security vulnerabilities that could have potentially led to a data breach. These vulnerabilities were scheduled to be remediated by September 2013, but still remain open and unaddressed today.

Unfortunately, the overdue remediation of known vulnerabilities for e-QIP is only a single example of a more widespread problem at OPM. Both our FY 2012 and FY 2013 FISMA reports indicated that out of OPM's 47 major information systems, 22 had known vulnerabilities with remediation activity greater than 120 days overdue. In FY 2014, the number grew to 38.

This issue demonstrates the importance of the Authorization process (as discussed above), but is also an example of OPM's historical neglect of IT security. The agency has failed to complete system Authorizations for its most sensitive systems, but even when the agency has known about security vulnerabilities, it has failed to take action.

OPM's Infrastructure Improvement Project

In April 2014, in response to the March 2014 breach, OPM initiated a major IT overhaul (referred to as the Project). The initial plan was to make major security improvements to the existing environment and continue to operate OPM systems in their current location. During the process of implementing security upgrades, OPM determined that it would be more effective to completely overhaul the agency's IT infrastructure and architecture and move it into an entirely new environment (referred to as the Shell).

On June 17, 2015, we issued a Flash Audit Alert detailing concerns related to project management as well as the use of a sole source contract for the entire Project. OPM provided a written response to our Flash Audit Alert on June 22, 2015. Below is a brief description of some of our specific concerns, as well as OPM's response.

- Missing planning documentation: As per OMB requirements, the agency must prepare a Major IT Business Case proposal (formerly known as an Exhibit 300) for a project of this size and scope. This document requires that the agency fully evaluate the costs, benefits, and risks associated with the Project. In response to our Flash Audit Alert, OPM officials stated that an overarching Major IT Business Case proposal is not necessary since they view the various phases of this project as extensions of existing IT investments established by previous Major IT Business Case proposals. OPM officials also objected to the amount of time required to complete such a proposal since it would negatively impact their implementation plans.

  We disagree with this view because this is a new project creating an entirely new IT infrastructure and architecture. Many of OPM's approximately 350 major and minor IT systems will need to be completely redesigned to be compatible with the new environment. This is clearly a major initiative that requires a Major IT Business Case proposal, especially to fund the migration effort. In addition, the process of creating the proposal, and the related artifacts that are generated during the effort, will serve as an invaluable project management tool throughout the life cycle of the Project.

- Best practices and requirements not followed: OPM officials have also failed to follow industry best practices as well as OPM's own System Development Life Cycle requirements for basic project management activities and documents. On July 1, 2015, OPM officials provided a status of their progress in preparing some of these items. Most of the activities and documents, which should have been completed prior to the Project's initiation, have still not been completed.

- Lack of a complete inventory: In order to determine the capabilities and functions that the new IT environment would have to perform, OPM first needs a complete list of all of the IT systems that will have to be housed on the new platform. OPM has a plan in place to develop such an inventory, but it is not yet complete.

- <u>Lack of comprehensive cost estimate</u>: OPM had estimated that the cost of the Project would be $93 million, but this estimate does *not* include the costs of migrating all of the agency's existing IT systems to the new Shell. This will be, by far, the most costly part of the Project. However, without a complete inventory of all of the IT systems that need to be migrated, OPM cannot develop a reliable cost estimate. To compare, when OPM had to migrate a single system (its financial system) to a new cloud-based environment, it took two years and approximately $30 million to complete. This Project is much larger, involving approximately 350 major and minor systems.

- <u>No dedicated funding stream</u>: Another related concern is that there is no dedicated funding stream for the entire Project, creating a very high risk that funding will be inadequate to support the complete migration effort. When combined with our serious concerns about the lack of a disciplined project management approach, the failure to identify a funding stream for the Project creates a high risk that the Project will fail to meet its stated objectives of creating a more secure IT environment at a lower cost.

- <u>Use of a sole-source contract</u>: Our review of procurement documents and discussions with senior OPM officials indicated that they plan to use a sole-source contract for the entire Project. We agree that the initial phase of the Project (immediately strengthening OPM's IT infrastructure in response to the March 2014 breach) was a quick response to an emergency, and thus use of a sole-source contract was appropriate. However, the later phases of the Project are not urgent and the contracts for those services should be subject to full and open competition. Moreover, it should be noted that the later phases of the Project, such as the migration of systems to the Shell, require a wide array of skill sets. It is highly unlikely that a single vendor could provide all of the necessary services for the migration effort.

  Although OPM has publicly stated that the sole-source contract was intended only for the first two phases of the Project, it was clearly indicated in the documents we reviewed, as well as during discussions with the OCIO, that the contract was intended to cover the entire Project. If OPM now plans to use full and open competition for the remainder of this effort, we welcome this new approach. We will continue to monitor the use of the sole-source contract to ensure that OPM complies with appropriate regulations.

We are currently working with OPM to obtain additional information regarding these issues. The OIG will continue to monitor the progress of this Project and communicate any concerns we may have, both in writing and in meetings with OPM officials. We hope that the agency will address the significant deficiencies we have identified because if they do not, we believe that the Project has a high risk of failure.

Conclusion

As discussed above, OPM has a history of struggling to comply with FISMA requirements. Although some areas have improved, such as the centralization of IT security responsibility within the OCIO, other problems persist. Until OPM's security weaknesses are resolved, OPM systems will continue to be an inviting target for attackers.

If OPM's new modernization project is implemented appropriately, we believe that it will significantly improve OPM's IT operations, including its IT security posture. However, there are several issues, including significant budgetary concerns, which must be addressed. If they are not, we fear that there is a high risk this project will fail to meet its stated objectives.

Thank you for your time and I am happy to answer any questions you may have.

32

UNITED STATES OFFICE OF PERSONNEL MANAGEMENT
1900 E STREET NW, WASHINGTON, DC 20415

BIOGRAPHY

Michael R. Esser

Michael R. Esser was appointed Assistant Inspector General for Audits and to the Senior Executive Service in April 2006. Mr. Esser is responsible for overseeing the Office of Audits in conducting audits and special reviews of programs administered by the U.S. Office of Personnel Management, the largest of which are the Federal Employees Health Benefits Program (FEHBP), the Civil Service Retirement System and the Federal Employees Retirement System, and the Federal Investigative Services.   His office also conducts audits of the Federal Employees' Group Life Insurance Program; Federal Employees Dental Vision Program; Flexible Spending Account Program; Federal Long Term Care Program; the agency's information systems, as well as information systems of the health carriers participating in the FEHBP.

Mr. Esser joined the Office of the Inspector General in February 1991 as an auditor, working primarily on the audits of the agency's consolidated financial statements. In November 2002, he was selected as the Chief of the Internal Audits Group, with responsibility for all audits of the agency's internal programs. Prior to coming to the U.S. Office of Personnel Management, Mr. Esser spent one year with a Northern Virginia CPA firm, and five years with Town & Country Mortgage Corporation in Fairfax, Virginia, the last three years of which was as Controller.

He attended George Mason University, graduating in 1984 with a Bachelor of Science degree in Accounting, and going on to earn a Masters in Business Administration in 1986.   He is a member of the American Institute of Certified Public Accountants.

33

Chairwoman COMSTOCK. Thank you.

And I now recognize Mr. Snell for five minutes to present his testimony.

TESTIMONY OF MR. DAVID SNELL, DIRECTOR, FEDERAL BENEFITS SERVICE DEPARTMENT, NATIONAL ACTIVE AND RETIRED FEDERAL EMPLOYEES ASSOCIATION

Mr. SNELL. Thank you. Good afternoon and thank you for inviting me to testify. I appreciate the opportunity to express NARFE's views regarding the recent data breaches at the Office of Personnel Management, OPM. We are deeply concerned over the failure of the federal government to protect its personnel computer systems and the devastating impact the recent breaches of these systems may have on national security, as well as on the financial and personal security of millions of current and former federal employees.

Let me be clear. The potential consequences of these breaches are severe. The personal records obtained through the data breaches include the highly personal and sensitive information of millions of current and former employees and even applicants for federal employment. The extent of the breaches is enormous, likely reaching beyond 18 million individuals.

Possession of the information contained in the Standard Form 86, a 120-page security clearance form containing an applicant's life history, could give our enemies the means to attempt to corrupt or blackmail government employees and compromise military and intelligence secrets. Moreover, it could make public servants vulnerable to grave risks to their personal security and that of their families and loved ones.

While the perpetrators of this act bear the obvious and primary fault in this matter, the federal government, including both the Administration and Congress, has an obligation to do its best to protect the sensitive information its employees and job applicants are required to disclose as a condition of employment. It failed to meet that obligation.

Despite explicit warnings by Inspectors General since 1997, OPM failed to put in place adequate safeguards for both its aged and newer computer systems. This permitted the theft of massive amounts of personally identifiable information. Even now, the current OPM Inspector General issued a flash audit of OPM's plans to improve its data security and found them to have ''a very high risk of project failure.''

Our government has failed its employees. It is imperative to act swiftly and ensure an incident of this magnitude does not repeat itself. The Congressional oversight and response, including this hearing, is a good start, but we need continued vigilant efforts to improve the federal government's information technology and data security for the future.

The federal government, including both the Administration and Congress, now has an obligation to remedy to the best of its ability what has transpired. This should have started with effective communication with federal employees, retirees, and others affected by the breaches and the organizations that represent them. Unfortunately, communications has fallen short of expectations. While

OPM has provided notice to those affected by the breach announced June 4 and has communicated with organizations in that regard, it has thus far failed in its basic duty to inform individuals affected by the second and more troubling breach announced June 12 and continues to fail to answer many important questions about both breaches. The failure of OPM to safeguard personal information should not be compounded by deflecting questions.

Our written testimony details many of the questions we are still seeking answers to regarding the details of exactly what data has been accessed. The federal community and everyone affected by the data have been—data breach deserves answers to these questions.

In addition, to better communication, the federal government should provide lifetime credit monitoring and additional identity theft insurance. The 18 months of credit monitoring offered by OPM is woefully inadequate. The depth of personal information exposed is enormous and the threat to individuals extends way beyond 18 months. It is only fair to provide financial protection in line with the threat that has been posed. Furthermore, Congress should appropriate funds necessary to provide this protection.

The question posed in the title of this hearing ''Is This the Tip of the Iceberg?'' is a valid one. While I cannot answer that, I will say I certainly hope not. The recent breaches should be a wake-up call to this country and its leaders about the dangers of cyber terrorism and the critical need to protect our government's core functions. Let's make sure this isn't the tip of the iceberg but rather the last time our federal government has to deal with cybersecurity breach that threatens the financial security of its employees.

Thank you again for the opportunity to share our views.

[The prepared statement of Mr. Snell follows:]

WRITTEN TESTIMONY BY
DAVID SNELL
FEDERAL BENEFITS SERVICE DIRECTOR
NATIONAL ACTIVE AND RETIRED FEDERAL EMPLOYEES ASSOCIATION

BEFORE
UNITED STATES HOUSE OF REPRESENTATIVES
COMMITTEE ON SCIENCE, SPACE, AND TECHNOLOGY

SUBCOMMITTEE ON RESEARCH AND TECHNOLOGY

AND

SUBCOMMITTEE ON OVERSIGHT

HEARING TITLED
"IS THE OPM DATA BREACH THE TIP OF THE ICEBERG?"

July 8, 2015

Chairwoman Comstock, Chairman Loudermilk, Ranking Member Lipinski, Ranking Member Beyer, and Subcommittee members:

On behalf of the five million federal workers and annuitants represented by the National Active and Retired Federal Employees Association (NARFE), I appreciate the opportunity to express our views regarding the recent data breaches at the Office of Personnel Management (OPM) and its implications for current, former and prospective federal employees.

We are deeply concerned over the failure of the federal government to adequately protect its personnel computer systems and the devastating impact the recent breaches of these systems may have on national security, as well as on the financial and personal security of millions of current and former federal employees.

Make no mistake: The potential consequences of these breaches are severe. The personnel records obtained through the data breaches include the highly personal and sensitive information of millions of current and former employees, and even applicants for federal employment. The extent of the breaches is enormous, likely reaching beyond 18 million individuals.

Possession of the information contained in the SF-86, the security clearance form data exposed by the latest incursion, could give our enemies the means to attempt to corrupt or blackmail government employees, compromise military and intelligence secrets, and even recruit Americans to join or assist terrorist organizations. Moreover, it could lead to the possibility that particular public servants would become vulnerable to grave risks that could threaten their personal security and that of their families and loved ones.

While the perpetrators of this act bear the obvious and primary fault in this matter, the federal government – including both the Administration and Congress – has an obligation to do its best to adequately protect the sensitive information its employees and job applicants are required to disclose as a condition of employment. It failed to meet that obligation.

Despite explicit warnings by inspectors general since 1997, OPM continually failed to put in place adequate safeguards for both its aged and newer computer systems. Through acts of omission and commission, the agency permitted the theft of massive amounts of personally identifiable information. Even now, as OPM works to remedy the situation, the current OPM inspector general issued a flash audit of OPM's plans to improve its data security and found them to have a "very high risk of project failure."

Our government has failed its employees. It is imperative that we not only act swiftly to remedy this situation, but we must also ensure an incident of this magnitude does not repeat itself. We must do a better job of protecting the millions of federal employees who serve this nation. The congressional oversight and response, including this hearing, is a good start. But we must become even more vigilant in our efforts to improve the federal government's information technology and data security to ensure that such a massive and damaging breach never happens again.

Improve Communication to Federal Employees and Retirees

The federal government – including both the Administration and Congress – now has an obligation to correct, to the best of its ability, what has transpired. This should have started with effective communication with federal employees, retirees, others affected by the breaches and the organizations that represent them. Unfortunately, communication has fallen short of expectations.

While OPM has provided notice to those affected by the breach announced on June 4, and has communicated with organizations in that regard, it has thus far failed in its basic duty to inform individuals affected by the second and more troubling breach, announced June 12, and continues to fail to answer many important questions about both breaches.

The OPM website with Frequently Asked Questions on the cyberattack has barely been updated since June 4. Federal employee and retiree representatives learned about the second breach from the news media, not from the Administration. It has been nearly four weeks since the second breach was announced, and we have yet to receive *any* information from the Administration on this incident. The lack of information from an official source has fueled rumors and exacerbated the unease of federal employees and retirees and their friends and families.

The failure of OPM to adequately safeguard the personal information of federal employees, retirees, prospective employees and their families should not be compounded by deflecting questions, the answers to which would benefit both active and retired federal employees. We call on OPM to provide the very information that the perpetrators of this crime already have. Notably, NARFE continues to seek answers to the following questions.

As it relates to the first breach announced on June 4, 2015:

- Why were only some retirees affected in the first breach?

- Which, if any, federal agency personnel records were not included in those that were accessed?

- Is there a specific date before which the employment records would **not** be included in those accessed? And a closely related question: How long does OPM retain employment information after someone has retired?

- Given the insecurity of the Internet, how can an affected party know for certain that the outreach they are receiving at OPM's direction from a commercial source (CSID) is, in fact, legitimate? Why are PINs and other information being sent via email from a non-government email address? One of our members asked: "How can I be sure this email is really from CSID?"

- After the June 4 announcement, OPM repeatedly stated that it does not keep congressional or legislative branch employment data, yet several individuals who work or have worked on Capitol Hill have received notification that their personal information has been exposed. To what extent does OPM maintain legislative branch employment data?

- Notifications are being sent to individuals who have died since leaving federal service. How can their next of kin take action? What if no one related to the deceased is living at the last known address? How will next of kin be notified? The answer provided on the OPM website in this regard is insufficient and unhelpful.

- We are receiving reports that individuals logging in to the website with their PIN and username are getting someone else's information. Is this issue widespread? Is this issue being fixed?

- Will those affected be asked to provide their Social Security number once they provide their PIN over the phone? We have received reports of this, which is making individuals uneasy.

As it relates to the second breach announced on June 12, the questions are endless. However, in particular, NARFE members would like to know if retirement records were exposed in the second hack. These records contain bank account information and annuity identification numbers.

The federal community and everyone affected by this breach deserve answers to these questions.

Provide Credit Monitoring and Identity Theft Insurance

The financial credit reporting measures OPM has offered to those whose information has been compromised are woefully inadequate. Protection should logically and fairly meet the scope of the threat to federal employees and retirees.

In light of the magnitude of the records breached, the nature of the information compromised, and the potential for a lifetime of identity theft and fraud, the federal government should offer free credit monitoring services for the lifetime of anyone affected and increase the amount of identity theft insurance provided (in specific circumstances, unlimited coverage may be required). It may be years before the information taken is used by criminals, and it is only fair to provide continued financial protection for the many victims who spent a lifelong career in federal service.

Congress should provide the appropriations necessary to provide adequate credit and identity theft protection for the federal employees and retirees affected.

Conclusion

The question posed in the title of this hearing, "Is this the tip of the iceberg?" is a valid one. While I cannot answer that, I will say: I certainly hope not. We have seen cybersecurity breaches at the U.S. Postal Service, the contractor USIS, the Department of Energy and the Department of

Homeland Security. If the OPM security breaches are the tip of the iceberg, we have challenging times ahead of us.

The recent breaches should be a wake-up call to this country and its leaders about the dangers of cyberterrorism and the critical need to protect our government's core functions. In preparing for the future, it is necessary for our leaders to properly evaluate how we ended up in this situation yet again. It also is incumbent on Congress to ensure federal agencies have the necessary resources to ensure a breach of this magnitude does not reoccur. Let's make sure this isn't the tip of the iceberg, but rather the last time our federal government has to deal with a cybersecurity breach that threatens the financial security of its employees.

Thank you again for the opportunity to share our views with you.

Biography – David B. Snell

David B. Snell is the director of the Federal Benefits Services Department at the National Active and Retired Federal Employees Association, providing insight and analysis on the application and rules of federal employee and retiree benefits. Snell is frequently quoted on federal issues, including retirement processing and the retirement claims backlog at the Office of Personnel Management (OPM), the Federal Employee Health Benefits Program, Thrift Savings Plan, Medicare and Social Security.

In 2012, Snell testified before Congress on behalf of the 30-member Federal-Postal Coalition on federal employees' retirement security. A frequent guest on the WTOP radio show *Your Turn with Mike Causey*, Snell is a trusted advisor to a wide audience on benefit issues that affect federal employees and retirees.

Prior to joining NARFE, Mr. Snell worked for nearly three decades at the Office of Personnel Management. His last position was chief of the Retirement Benefits Branch, where he oversaw the annual Open Season for annuitants and the annual mailings for the annuitant tax season.

A veteran, Snell served four years in the U.S. Air Force and holds a Bachelor of Science degree from George Mason University in Fairfax, VA.

Chairwoman COMSTOCK. Thank you, Mr. Snell.

And now, Dr. Romine, for five minutes for your testimony.

TESTIMONY OF DR. CHARLES ROMINE, DIRECTOR, INFORMATION TECHNOLOGY LABORATORY, NATIONAL INSTITUTE OF STANDARDS AND TECHNOLOGY

Dr. ROMINE. Chairwoman Comstock, Chairman Loudermilk, Ranking Member Lipinski, Ranking Member Beyer, and Members of the Subcommittees, I'm Dr. Charles Romine, Director of the Information Technology Laboratory at NIST. Thank you for the opportunity to appear before you today to discuss our responsibilities for assisting federal agencies with cybersecurity.

NIST has worked in cybersecurity with federal agencies, industry, and academia since 1972. Our role, to research, develop, and deploy information security standards and technology to protect information systems against threats to the confidentiality, integrity, and availability of information and services was strengthened through the Computer Security Act of 1987, broadened through the Federal Information Security Management Act of 2002 or FISMA, and reaffirmed in the Federal Information Security Modernization Act of 2014.

NIST carries out its responsibilities under FISMA through the creation of a series of Federal Information Processing Standards, or FIPS, and associated guidelines. Under FISMA agencies are required to implement those FIPS. To further assist agencies, NIST provides management, operational, and technical security guidelines covering a broad range of cybersecurity topics.

NIST has a series of specific responsibilities in FISMA to—of particular relevance to today's hearing were addressed by NIST and published as FIPS 199, the standard for security categorization of federal information and information systems; and FIPS 200, which sets the minimum security requirements based on the categorization identified using FIPS 199.

NIST created baselines for these minimum security requirements based on three levels determined in accordance with FIPS 199: low, moderate, and high. For example, at a high categorization, FIPS 199 states that "the loss of confidentiality, integrity, or availability could be expected to have a severe or catastrophic adverse effect on organizational operations, organizational assets, or individuals."

Examples of controls included in the associated baselines then cover a range of requirements for a lifecycle of security. For example, security awareness and training, contingency planning, access control, system disposal, and incident response. Once a baseline is established, NIST provides guidance to agencies to assist in determining that the baseline is adequate to meet their risk-based requirements.

An agency may need to enhance a given baseline to address local risks, the agency's mission, and technical infrastructure. For example, an agency with a real-time monitoring system such as workstations in air traffic control or critical patient monitoring systems might not want to use a timed password-locked screensaver to mitigate security issues for unattended workstations. Instead, a guard or site surveillance system might be more appropriate to support the mission and still meet the intent of the baseline.

Establishing a sound security baseline is not the end of security for an agency. NIST provides standards, guidelines, and tools for agencies to test and assess their security and continuously monitor their implementation and new risks. The authorization of a system by a management official is an important quality control under FISMA. By authorizing a system, the manager formally assumes responsibility for operating a system at an acceptable level of risk to the agency operations or individuals.

Under FISMA, NIST does not assess ,audit, or test agency security implementations. Congress recognized that placing such responsibilities on NIST would impede its ability to work with federal agency and private-sector stakeholders to develop standards, guidelines, and practices in the open, transparent, and collaborative manner that Congress intended.

NIST's statutory role as the developer but not the enforcer of standards and guidelines under FISMA have ensured NIST's ongoing ability to engage freely and positively with federal agencies on the implementation challenges and issues they experience in using these standards and guidelines. NIST is committed to continue to help agency officials address their responsibilities under FISMA to understand and mitigate risks to their information and information systems that could adversely affect their missions.

We recognize that we have an essential responsibility in cybersecurity and in helping industry, consumers, and government to counter cybersecurity threats. Active collaboration within the public sector and between the public and private sectors is the only way to effectively meet this challenge leveraging each participant's roles, responsibilities, and capabilities.

Thank you for the opportunity to testify today on NIST's work in federal cybersecurity and I would be happy to answer any questions that you may have.

[The prepared statement of Dr. Romine follows:]

Testimony of

Charles H. Romine, Ph.D.

Director
Information Technology Laboratory
National Institute of Standards and Technology
United States Department of Commerce

Before the
United States House of Representatives
Committee on Science, Space and Technology
Subcommittee on Research and Technology and
Subcommittee on Oversight

"Is the OPM Data Breach the Tip of the Iceberg?"

July 8, 2015

Introduction

Chairwoman Comstock, Chairman Loudermilk, Ranking Member Lipinski, Ranking Member Beyer, and members of the Subcommittees, I am Dr. Charles Romine, the Director of the Information Technology Laboratory (ITL) at the Department of Commerce's National Institute of Standards and Technology (NIST). Thank you for the opportunity to appear before you today to discuss one of our key roles in cybersecurity. Specifically, today I will testify about our responsibilities for assisting federal agencies with cybersecurity.

The Role of NIST in Cybersecurity

With programs focused on national priorities from the Smart Grid and electronic health records to forensics, atomic clocks, advanced nanomaterials, computer chips and more, NIST's overall mission is to promote U.S. innovation and industrial competitiveness by advancing measurement science, standards, and technology in ways that enhance economic security and improve our quality of life.

In the area of cybersecurity, NIST has worked with federal agencies, industry, and academia since 1972, starting with the development of the Data Encryption Standard, when the potential commercial benefit of this technology became clear. Our role, to research, develop, and deploy information security standards and technology to protect information systems against threats to the confidentiality, integrity, and availability of information and services, was strengthened through the Computer Security Act of 1987, broadened through the Federal Information Security Management Act of 2002 (FISMA) and reaffirmed in the Federal Information Security Modernization Act of 2014.

Our Role under FISMA

At the time of the original FISMA bill, *House Report 107-787* stated the importance of NIST's approach to developing successful standards, guidelines and practices:

> ". . . open, transparent standards activities undertaken by NIST, such as the development and publication of the Advanced Encryption Standard, promote flexibility by permitting alternative hardware and software solutions to provide equivalent levels of protection and enable vendors to offer a variety of solutions to meet customer needs. By contrast, when standards development has not been open and the resulting NIST standard is not published and flexibly implementable, the standard has failed to gain broad acceptance and use."

NIST carries out its responsibilities under FISMA through the creation of a series of Federal Information Processing Standards (FIPS) and associated guidelines and practices. Under FISMA, federal agencies are required to implement these FIPS. NIST provides management, operational, and technical security guidelines for Federal agencies covering a broad range of topics, such as protecting the confidentiality of Controlled Unclassified Information (CUI) while residing in nonfederal information systems and organizations, BIOS management and measurement, key management and derivation, media sanitization, electronic authentication, security automation, Bluetooth and wireless protocols, incident handling and intrusion detection, malware, cloud computing, public key infrastructure, risk assessments, supply chain risk management, authentication, access control, security automation and continuous monitoring.

Beyond these documents - which are peer-reviewed throughout industry, government, and academia - NIST conducts workshops, awareness briefings, and outreach to ensure comprehension of standards and guidelines, to share ongoing and planned activities, and to aid in scoping guidelines in a collaborative, open, and transparent manner.

NIST has a series of very specific responsibilities called for in both the Federal Information Security Management and Modernization Acts, including the development of:

- A standard for categorizing information to be used by all federal agencies. The categories are based on the potential impact of harm to the organization if the information or information systems are compromised; and
- Minimum security requirements (*i.e.*, management, operational, and technical controls), for each information category.

In support of FISMA implementation, in recent years NIST has strengthened its collaboration with the Department of Defense, the Intelligence Community, and the Committee on National Security Systems, through the Joint Task Force Transformation Initiative, which continues to develop key cybersecurity guidelines for protecting federal information and information systems.

This collaboration allows for a broad-based and comprehensive set of safeguards and countermeasures for information systems. This unified framework provides a standardized method for expressing security at all levels, from operational implementation to compliance reporting. It allows for an environment of information sharing and interconnections among these communities and significantly reduces costs, time, and resources needed for finite sets of systems and administrators to report on cybersecurity to multiple authorities.

Federal Information Processing Standards and Mandatory Baselines

Of particular relevance to today's hearing are two FIPS developed by NIST to meet the specific requirements under FISMA:

- FIPS 199, the standard for security categorization of federal information and information systems; and

- FIPS 200, which sets minimum security requirements based on those categorization.

The minimum security requirements of FIPS 200 comprise a set of security controls that vary in breadth and depth depending on the importance of the information and information system to the mission of the agency.

NIST created three baselines for these minimum security requirements based on three categorization levels determined in accordance with FIPS 199: low, moderate, and high. These baselines are specified in our guideline documents and available tools. For example, at a "high" categorization, FIPS 199 states that "[t]he loss of confidentiality, integrity, or availability could be expected to have a severe or catastrophic adverse effect on organizational operations, organizational assets, or individuals."[1]

Examples of controls included in the associated baselines then cover a range of requirements for a lifecycle of security for any agency. Some specific examples include: security awareness and training; contingency planning; access controls; incident identification; incident response; and system disposal. Some controls call for specific technical implementations as well, such as the use of encryption, Domain Network Security Protocols, port locking, and white listing. Through an open and transparent process, these baselines are developed and updated collaboratively with our partners in government and industry.

Once a baseline is established, NIST provides guidance to agencies to assist them in determining that the baseline is adequate to meet their risk-based requirements. An agency may need to enhance a given baseline to address local risks and take into account that agency's mission and technical infrastructure. This enhancement might require that an agency substitute a specific control for another appropriate security mechanism.

For example, an agency with a real time monitoring system such as workstations in Air Traffic Control, pipe line pressure monitoring or critical patient monitoring systems might not want to use a timed, password locked screen saver to mitigate security issues for unattended workstations. Instead, use of a guard or site surveillance systems might be more appropriate to support the mission, and would allow that agency to meet the intent of the requirement in the baseline. In other words, while a

---

[1] The standard further amplifies this definition for agencies as follows: "A severe or catastrophic adverse effect means that, for example, the loss of confidentiality, integrity, or availability might: (i) cause a severe degradation in or loss of mission capability to an extent and duration that the organization is not able to perform one or more of its primary functions; (ii) result in major damage to organizational assets; (iii) result in major financial loss; or (iv) result in severe or catastrophic harm to individuals involving loss of life or serious life threatening injuries."

specific step recommended in the baseline may not fit an agency's needs, a complementary and compensating step can achieve the desired security outcome.

Establishing a sound security baseline is not the end of security for an agency, just as developing an IT system is not the end of an IT project. NIST provides standards, guidelines and tools for agencies to test and assess their security and then to continuously monitor their implementation and new risks. This process is essential to ensure the baseline is initially implemented correctly and remains appropriate as technologies, threats, and missions evolve. We stress that the authorization of a system by a management official is an important quality control under FISMA. By authorizing processing in a system, the manager accepts the associated risk. This causes that official to formally assume responsibility for operating an information system at an acceptable level of risk to agency operations, agency assets, or individuals.

Complying with FISMA

Under FISMA, NIST does not assess, audit, or test agency security implementations. Similarly, Congress has not accorded NIST with oversight authority. Congress recognized that placing such responsibilities on NIST would impede and ultimately defeat its ability to work with federal agency and private sector stakeholders to develop standards, guidelines and practices in the open, transparent, and collaborative manner Congress intended, as noted above in my testimony.

Accordingly, compliance and oversight authority resides with other agencies, such as OMB. Federal agency heads, in coordination with their Chief Information Officers and Senior Agency Information Security Officers, report the security status of their information systems to OMB in accordance with annual FISMA reporting guidance. In addition, agency Inspectors General provide an independent assessment of the security status of federal information systems, also reporting results to OMB annually.

NIST's statutory role as the developer – but not the enforcer – of standards and guidelines under FISMA has ensured NIST's ongoing ability to engage freely and positively with federal agencies on the implementation challenges and issues they experience in using these standards and guidelines. We meet frequently with agencies and hold regular Federal Security Manager Forums to discuss these issues, our standards and guidance, share lessons learned, and gain insights into methods and means to continually improve our standards, guidelines, and practices.

Conclusion

NIST is committed to continue to help agency officials address their responsibilities under FISMA to understand and mitigate risks to their information and information systems that could adversely affect their missions. We recognize that we have an essential responsibility in cybersecurity and in helping industry, consumers, and government to counter cybersecurity threats. Our work in the areas of information security, trusted networks, and software quality is applicable to a wide variety of organizations, and is leveraged by industry and governments throughout the world. Active collaboration within the public sector, and between the public and private sectors, is the only way to effectively meet this challenge, leveraging each participant's roles, responsibilities, and capabilities.

Thank you for the opportunity to testify today on NIST's work in federal cybersecurity. I would be happy to answer any questions you may have.

Charles H. Romine

Charles Romine is Director of the Information Technology Laboratory (ITL). ITL is one of seven research Laboratories within the National Institute of Standards and Technology (NIST) with an annual budget of $150 million, more than 440 employees, and about 150 guest researchers from industry, universities, and foreign laboratories.

Dr. Romine oversees a research program designed to promote U.S. innovation and industrial competitiveness by developing and disseminating standards, measurements, and testing for interoperability, security, usability, and reliability of information systems, including cybersecurity standards and guidelines for Federal agencies and U.S. industry, supporting these and measurement science at NIST through fundamental and applied research in computer science, mathematics, and statistics. Through its efforts, ITL supports NIST's mission to promote U.S. innovation and industrial competitiveness by advancing measurement science, standards, and technology in ways that enhance economic security and improve our quality of life.

Within NIST's traditional role as the overseer of the National Measurement System, ITL is conducting research addressing measurement challenges in information technology as well as issues of information and software quality, integrity, and usability. ITL is also charged with leading the nation in using existing and emerging IT to help meet national priorities, including developing cybersecurity standards, guidelines, and associated methods and techniques, cloud computing, electronic voting, smart grid, homeland security applications, and health information technology

Education:

Ph.D. in Applied Mathematics from the University of Virginia

B.A. in Mathematics from the University of Virginia.

Chairwoman COMSTOCK. Thank you, Doctor.

And I now recognize Mr. Wilshusen for five minutes to present his testimony.

TESTIMONY OF MR. GREGORY WILSHUSEN, DIRECTOR, INFORMATION SECURITY ISSUES, U.S. GOVERNMENT ACCOUNTABILITY OFFICE

Dr. WILSHUSEN. Chairman Comstock, Chairman Loudermilk, Ranking Members Lipinski and Beyer, and Members of the Subcommittees, thank you for the opportunity to testify at today's hearing.

The recent OPM data breaches affected millions of federal employees. However, OPM is by no means the only agency to suffer data breaches or face challenges securing its computer systems and information. The number of information security incidents both cyber and non-cyber reported by federal agencies continues to rise, increasing from about 5,500 in fiscal year 2006 to over 67,000 in fiscal year 2014. Similarly, the number of incidents involving personally identifiable information more than doubled in recent years to over 27,000 in fiscal year 2014. These incidents illustrate the need for stronger information security controls across the federal government.

Today, I will discuss several cyber threats to federal systems, cybersecurity challenges facing federal agencies, and governmentwide initiatives aimed at improving cybersecurity.

Before I begin, if I may, I'd like to recognize members of my team who are instrumental in developing my statement and some of the work underpinning it. With me today is Larry Crosland, an Assistant Director who led this body of work. I also want to recognize Brad Becker, Lee McCracken, Chris Businsky, Scott Pettis, who also made significant contributions.

Madam Chairwoman, Mr. Chairman, the federal government faces an array of cyber-based threats to its computer networks and systems. These threats include both targeted and untargeted attacks from a variety of sources, including criminal groups, hackers, disgruntled insiders, and foreign nations. These sources vary in terms of their capabilities, willingness to act, and motives, which can include seeking monetary gain or pursuing an economic, political, or economic advantage.

In the grip of these threats, most federal agencies face challenges securing their systems and networks. Agencies continue to have shortcomings in assessing risks, developing and implementing security controls, and monitoring results. For example, 19 of 24 agencies covered by the Chief Financial Officers Act reported that information security weaknesses were either significant deficiency or material weakness for financial reporting purposes. And the Inspectors General at 23 of these agencies cited information security as a major management challenge for their agency.

Agencies also need to provide better oversight of the security their contractor operator systems. Five of six agencies we reviewed did not consistently assess their contractors' information security practices and controls, resulting in security lapses.

Even with effective controls, security incidents and data breaches can still occur. Agencies need to react swiftly and appropriately when they do. However, seven agencies we reviewed had not consistently implemented key operational practices for responding to data breaches involving personal information. GAO and agency IGs have made hundreds of recommendations to assist agencies in addressing these and other challenges. Implementing these recommendations will help strengthen agencies' ability to protect their systems and information.

DHS and the Office of Management and Budget have also launched several governmentwide initiatives to enhance cybersecurity. One such initiative is requiring stronger authentication of users through the use of personal identity verification, or PIV cards. However, OMB recently reported that only 41 percent of agency user accounts at 23 civilian agencies required PIV cards for accessing agency system's.

Another initiative, the National Cybersecurity Protection System is intended to detect and prevent malicious network traffic from entering federal civilian networks. GAO is presently reviewing the implementation of this system. Our preliminary observations indicate that the systems intrusion detection and prevention capabilities may be useful but are also limited.

While governmentwide initiatives hold promise for bolstering the federal cybersecurity posture, no single technology or set of practices is sufficient to protect against all cyber threats. A multi-layered defense in-depth strategy that includes well-trained personnel, effective and consistently applied processes, and appropriate technologies is needed to better manage cyber risks.

This concludes my oral statement. I'd be happy to answer your questions.

[The prepared statement of Mr. Wilshusen follows:]

United States Government Accountability Office

Testimony

Before the Subcommittees on Research and Technology and Oversight, Committee on Science, Space, and Technology, House of Representatives

For Release on Delivery
Expected at 2:00 p.m. ET
Wednesday, July 8, 2015

INFORMATION SECURITY

Cyber Threats and Data Breaches Illustrate Need for Stronger Controls across Federal Agencies

Statement of Gregory C. Wilshusen,
Director, Information Security Issues

July 8, 2015

INFORMATION SECURITY

Cyber Threats and Data Breaches Illustrate Need for Stronger Controls across Federal Agencies

GAO Highlights

Highlights of GAO-15-758T, a testimony before the Subcommittees on Research and Technology and Oversight, Committee on Science, Space, and Technology, House of Representatives

Why GAO Did This Study

Effective cybersecurity for federal information systems is essential to preventing the loss of resources, the compromise of sensitive information, and the disruption of government operations. Since 1997, GAO has designated federal information security as a government-wide high-risk area, and in 2003 expanded this area to include computerized systems supporting the nation's critical infrastructure. Earlier this year, in GAO's high-risk update, the area was further expanded to include protecting the privacy of personal information that is collected, maintained, and shared by both federal and nonfederal entities.

This statement summarizes (1) cyber threats to federal systems, (2) challenges facing federal agencies in securing their systems and information, and (3) government-wide initiatives aimed at improving cybersecurity. In preparing this statement, GAO relied on its previously published and ongoing work in this area.

What GAO Recommends

In previous work, GAO and agency inspectors general have made hundreds of recommendations to assist agencies in addressing cybersecurity challenges. GAO has also made recommendations to improve government-wide initiatives.

View GAO-15-758T. For more information, contact Gregory C. Wilshusen at (202) 512-6244 or wilshuseng@gao.gov.

What GAO Found

Federal systems face an evolving array of cyber-based threats. These threats can be unintentional—for example, from equipment failure or careless or poorly trained employees; or intentional—targeted or untargeted attacks from criminals, hackers, adversarial nations, or terrorists, among others. Threat actors use a variety of attack techniques that can adversely affect federal information, computers, software, networks, or operations, potentially resulting in the disclosure, alteration, or loss of sensitive information; destruction or disruption of critical systems; or damage to economic and national security. These concerns are further highlighted by recent incidents involving breaches of sensitive data and the sharp increase in information security incidents reported by federal agencies over the last several years, which have risen from 5,503 in fiscal year 2006 to 67,168 in fiscal year 2014.

GAO has identified a number of challenges federal agencies face in addressing threats to their cybersecurity. For example, agencies have been challenged with designing and implementing risk-based cybersecurity programs, as illustrated by 19 of 24 major agencies declaring cybersecurity as a significant deficiency or material weakness for financial reporting purposes. Other challenges include:

- enhancing oversight of contractors providing IT services,
- improving security incident response activities,
- responding to breaches of personal information, and
- implementing cybersecurity programs at small agencies.

Until federal agencies take actions to address these challenges—including implementing the hundreds of recommendations GAO and agency inspectors general have made—federal systems and information will be at an increased risk of compromise from cyber-based attacks and other threats.

Several government-wide initiatives are under way to bolster cybersecurity.

- **Personal Identity Verification:** The President and the Office of Management and Budget (OMB) directed agencies to issue credentials with enhanced security features to control access to federal facilities and systems. OMB recently reported that only 41 percent of user accounts at 23 civilian agencies had required these credentials to access agency systems.
- **Continuous Diagnostics and Mitigation:** This program is to provide agencies with tools for continuously monitoring cybersecurity risks. The Department of State adopted a continuous monitoring program, and GAO reported on the benefits and challenges in implementing the program.
- **National Cybersecurity Protection System:** This system is to provide capabilities for monitoring network traffic and detecting and preventing intrusions. GAO has ongoing work reviewing the system's implementation. Preliminary observations indicate that implementation of the intrusion detection and prevention capabilities may be limited and requirements for future capabilities appear to have not been fully defined.

While these initiatives are intended to improve security, no single technology or tool is sufficient to protect against all cyber threats. Rather, agencies need to employ a multi-layered approach to security that includes well-trained personnel, effective and consistently applied processes, and appropriate technologies.

_____ United States Government Accountability Office

Chairwoman Comstock, Chairman Loudermilk, Ranking Members Lipinski and Beyer, and Members of the Subcommittees:

Thank you for inviting me to testify at today's hearing on data breaches at the Office of Personnel Management (OPM) and cybersecurity challenges faced by federal agencies. As you know, the federal government faces an array of cyber-based threats to its systems and data, as illustrated by the recently reported data breaches at OPM, which affected millions of current and former federal employees. Such incidents underscore the urgent need for effective implementation of information security controls at federal agencies.

Since 1997, we have designated federal information security as a government-wide high-risk area, and in 2003 expanded this area to include computerized systems supporting the nation's critical infrastructure. Most recently, in the February 2015 update to our high-risk list, we further expanded this area to include protecting the privacy of personally identifiable information (PII)[1]—that is, personal information that is collected, maintained, and shared by both federal and nonfederal entities.[2]

My statement today will discuss (1) cyber threats facing federal systems, (2) challenges that federal agencies face in securing their systems and information, and (3) government-wide initiatives aimed at improving agencies' cybersecurity. In preparing this statement, we relied on our previous work in these areas, as well as the preliminary observations from our ongoing review of the Department of Homeland Security's (DHS) National Cybersecurity Protection System (NCPS) initiative. We discussed these observations with DHS officials. The prior reports cited throughout this statement contain detailed discussions of the scope of the work and the methodology used to carry it out. All the work on which this statement is based was conducted or is being conducted in accordance with generally accepted government auditing standards. Those standards require that we plan and perform audits to obtain sufficient, appropriate

---

[1]Personally identifiable information is information about an individual, including information that can be used to distinguish or trace an individual's identity, such as name, Social Security number, mother's maiden name, or biometric records, and any other personal information that is linked or linkable to an individual.

[2]See GAO, *High-Risk Series: An Update*, GAO-15-290 (Washington, D.C.: Feb. 11, 2015).

evidence to provide a reasonable basis for our findings and conclusions based on our audit objectives. We believe that the evidence obtained provides a reasonable basis for our findings and conclusions based on our audit objectives.

Background

As computer technology has advanced, both government and private entities have become increasingly dependent on computerized information systems to carry out operations and to process, maintain, and report essential information. Public and private organizations rely on computer systems to transmit proprietary and other sensitive information, develop and maintain intellectual capital, conduct operations, process business transactions, transfer funds, and deliver services. In addition, the Internet has grown increasingly important to American businesses and consumers, serving as a medium for hundreds of billions of dollars of commerce each year, and has developed into an extended information and communications infrastructure that supports vital services such as power distribution, health care, law enforcement, and national defense.

Ineffective protection of these information systems and networks can result in a failure to deliver these vital services, and result in

- loss or theft of computer resources, assets, and funds;
- inappropriate access to and disclosure, modification, or destruction of sensitive information, such as national security information, PII, and proprietary business information;
- disruption of essential operations supporting critical infrastructure, national defense, or emergency services;
- undermining of agency missions due to embarrassing incidents that erode the public's confidence in government;
- use of computer resources for unauthorized purposes or to launch attacks on other systems;
- damage to networks and equipment; and
- high costs for remediation.

Recognizing the importance of these issues, Congress enacted laws intended to improve the protection of federal information and systems.

These laws include the *Federal Information Security Modernization Act of 2014* (FISMA),[3] which, among other things, authorizes DHS to (1) assist the Office of Management and Budget (OMB) with overseeing and monitoring agencies' implementation of security requirements; (2) operate the federal information security incident center; and (3) provide agencies with operational and technical assistance, such as that for continuously diagnosing and mitigating cyber threats and vulnerabilities. The act also reiterated the 2002 FISMA requirement for the head of each agency to provide information security protections commensurate with the risk and magnitude of the harm resulting from unauthorized access, use, disclosure, disruption, modification, or destruction of the agency's information or information systems.

In addition, the act continues the requirement for federal agencies to develop, document, and implement an agency-wide information security program. The program is to provide security for the information and information systems that support the operations and assets of the agency, including those provided or managed by another agency, contractor, or other source.

The Federal Government Faces an Evolving Array of Cyber-Based Threats

Risks to cyber-based assets can originate from unintentional or intentional threats. Unintentional threats can be caused by, among other things, natural disasters, defective computer or network equipment, and careless or poorly trained employees. Intentional threats include both targeted and untargeted attacks from a variety of sources, including criminal groups, hackers, disgruntled employees, foreign nations engaged in espionage and information warfare, and terrorists.

These adversaries vary in terms of their capabilities, willingness to act, and motives, which can include seeking monetary gain or a political, economic, or military advantage. For example, adversaries possessing sophisticated levels of expertise and significant resources to pursue their objectives—sometimes referred to as "advanced persistent threats"—pose increasing risks. Table 1 describes common cyber adversaries.

---

[3]The Federal Information Security Modernization Act of 2014 (Pub. L. No. 113-283, Dec. 18, 2014) (2014 FISMA) largely superseded the very similar Federal Information Security Management Act of 2002 (Title III, Pub. L. No. 107-347, Dec. 17, 2002) (2002 FISMA).

57

Table 1: Common Cyber Adversaries

Threat source	Description
Bot-network operators	Bot-net operators use a network, or bot-net, of compromised, remotely controlled systems to coordinate attacks and to distribute phishing schemes, spam, and malware attacks. The services of these networks are sometimes made available on underground markets (e.g., purchasing a denial-of-service attack or services to relay spam or phishing attacks).
Criminal groups	Criminal groups seek to attack systems for monetary gain. Specifically, organized criminal groups use cyber exploits to commit identity theft, online fraud, and computer extortion. International corporate spies and criminal organizations also pose a threat to the United States through their ability to conduct industrial espionage and large-scale monetary theft and to hire or develop hacker talent.
Hackers/hacktivists	Hackers break into networks for the challenge, revenge, stalking, or monetary gain, among other reasons. Hacktivists are ideologically motivated actors who use cyber exploits to further political goals. While gaining unauthorized access once required a fair amount of skill or computer knowledge, hackers can now download attack scripts and protocols from the Internet and launch them against victim sites. Thus, while attack tools have become more sophisticated, they have also become easier to use. According to the Central Intelligence Agency, the large majority of hackers do not have the requisite expertise to threaten difficult targets such as critical U.S. networks. Nevertheless, the worldwide population of hackers poses a relatively high threat of an isolated or brief disruption causing serious damage.
Insiders	The disgruntled organization insider is a principal source of computer crime. Insiders may not need a great deal of knowledge about computer intrusions because their position within the organization often allows them to gain unrestricted access and cause damage to the targeted system or to steal system data. The insider threat includes contractors hired by the organization, as well as careless or poorly trained employees who may inadvertently introduce malware into systems.
Nations	Nations use cyber tools as part of their information-gathering and espionage activities. In addition, several nations are aggressively working to develop information warfare doctrine, programs, and capabilities. Such capabilities enable a single entity to potentially have a significant and serious impact by disrupting the supply, communications, and economic infrastructures that support military power—impacts that could affect the daily lives of citizens across the country. In his February 2015 testimony, the Director of National Intelligence stated that, among state actors, China, and Russia have highly sophisticated cyber programs, while Iran and North Korea have lesser technical capabilities but possibly more disruptive intent.
Terrorists	Terrorists seek to destroy, incapacitate, or exploit critical infrastructures in order to threaten national security, cause mass casualties, weaken the economy, and damage public morale and confidence. Terrorists may use phishing schemes or spyware/malware in order to generate funds or gather sensitive information.

Source: GAO analysis based on data from the Director of National Intelligence, Department of Justice, Central Intelligence Agency, and the Software Engineering Institute's CERT® Coordination Center. | GAO-15-758T

These adversaries make use of various techniques— or exploits—that may adversely affect federal information, computers, software, networks, and operations. Table 2 describes common types of cyber exploits.

Table 2: Types of Cyber Exploits

Type of exploit	Description
Cross-site scripting	An attack that uses third-party web resources to run script within the victim's web browser or scriptable application. This occurs when a browser visits a malicious website or clicks a malicious link. The most dangerous consequences occur when this method is used to exploit additional vulnerabilities that may permit an attacker to steal cookies (data exchanged between a web server and a browser), log key strokes, capture screen shots, discover and collect network information, and remotely access and control the victim's machine.
Denial-of-service/distributed denial-of-service	An attack that prevents or impairs the authorized use of networks, systems, or applications by exhausting resources. A distributed denial-of-service attack is a variant of the denial-of-service attack that uses numerous hosts to perform the attack.
Malware	Malware, also known as malicious code and malicious software, refers to a program that is inserted into a system, usually covertly, with the intent of compromising the confidentiality, integrity, or availability of the victim's data, applications, or operating system or otherwise annoying or disrupting the victim. Examples of malware include logic bombs, Trojan Horses, ransomware, viruses, and worms.
Phishing/spear phishing	A digital form of social engineering that uses authentic-looking, but fake, e-mails to request information from users or direct them to a fake website that requests information. Spear phishing is a phishing exploit that is targeted to a specific individual or group.
Passive wiretapping	The monitoring or recording of data, such as passwords transmitted in clear text, while they are being transmitted over a communications link. This is done without altering or affecting the data.
Spamming	Sending unsolicited commercial e-mail advertising for products, services, and websites. Spam can also be used as a delivery mechanism for malware and other cyber threats.
Spoofing	Creating a fraudulent website to mimic an actual, well-known website run by another party. E-mail spoofing occurs when the sender address and other parts of an e-mail header are altered to appear as though the e-mail originated from a different source.
Structured Query Language (SQL) injection	An attack that involves the alteration of a database search in a web-based application, which can be used to obtain unauthorized access to sensitive information in a database.
War driving	The method of driving through cities and neighborhoods with a wireless-equipped computer–sometimes with a powerful antenna–searching for unsecured wireless networks.
Zero-day exploit	An exploit that takes advantage of a security vulnerability previously unknown to the general public. In many cases, the exploit code is written by the same person who discovered the vulnerability. By writing an exploit for the previously unknown vulnerability, the attacker creates a potent threat since the compressed timeframe between public discoveries of both makes it difficult to defend against.

Source: GAO analysis of data from the National Institute of Standards and Technology, United States Computer Emergency Readiness Team, and industry reports; and GAO. | GAO-15-758T

An adversary may employ multiple tactics, techniques, and exploits to conduct a cyber attack. The National Institute of Standards and Technology (NIST) has identified several representative events that may constitute a cyber attack:[4]

---

[4]NIST, *Guide for Conducting Risk Assessments*, Special Publication 800-30, Revision 1 (Gaithersburg, Md.: September 2012).

- **Perform reconnaissance and gather information:** An adversary may gather information on a target by, for example, scanning its network perimeters or using publicly available information.

- **Craft or create attack tools:** An adversary prepares its means of attack by, for example, crafting a phishing attack or creating a counterfeit ("spoof") website.

- **Deliver, insert, or install malicious capabilities:** An adversary can use common delivery mechanisms, such as e-mail or downloadable software, to insert or install malware into its target's systems.

- **Exploit and compromise:** An adversary may exploit poorly configured, unauthorized, or otherwise vulnerable information systems to gain access.

- **Conduct an attack:** Attacks can include efforts to intercept information or disrupt operations (e.g., denial of service or physical attacks).

- **Achieve results:** Desired results include obtaining sensitive information via network "sniffing" or exfiltration, causing degradation or destruction of the target's capabilities; damaging the integrity of information through creating, deleting, or modifying data; or causing unauthorized disclosure of sensitive information.

- **Maintain a presence or set of capabilities:** An adversary may try to maintain an undetected presence on its target's systems by inhibiting the effectiveness of intrusion-detection capabilities or adapting behavior in response to the organization's surveillance and security measures.

More generally, the nature of cyber-based attacks can vastly enhance their reach and impact. For example, cyber attacks do not require physical proximity to their victims, can be carried out at high speeds and directed at multiple victims simultaneously, and can more easily allow attackers to remain anonymous. These inherent advantages, combined with the increasing sophistication of cyber tools and techniques, allow threat actors to target government agencies and their contractors, potentially resulting in the disclosure, alteration, or loss of sensitive information, including PII; theft of intellectual property; destruction or disruption of critical systems; and damage to economic and national security.

Since fiscal year 2006, the number of information security incidents affecting systems supporting the federal government has steadily increased each year: rising from 5,503 in fiscal year 2006 to 67,168 in fiscal year 2014, an increase of 1,121 percent. (See fig. 1.)

Figure 1: Incidents Reported to the U.S. Computer Emergency Readiness Team by Federal Agencies, Fiscal Years 2006 through 2014

Number of reported incidents

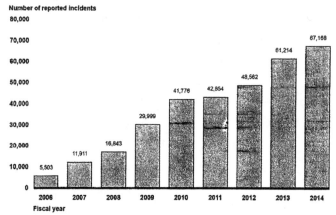

Source: GAO analysis of United States Computer Emergency Readiness Team data for fiscal years 2006-2014. | GAO-15-758T

Furthermore, the number of reported security incidents involving PII at federal agencies has more than doubled in recent years—from 10,481 incidents in fiscal year 2009 to 27,624 incidents in fiscal year 2014.

Figure 2 shows the different types of incidents reported in fiscal year 2014.

Figure 2: Information Security Incidents by Category, Fiscal Year 2014

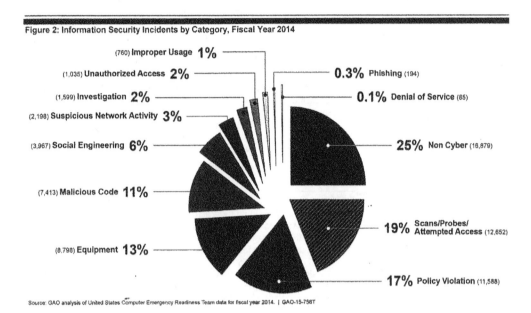

(760) Improper Usage **1%**

(1,035) Unauthorized Access **2%**

(1,599) Investigation **2%**

(2,198) Suspicious Network Activity **3%**

(3,967) Social Engineering **6%**

(7,413) Malicious Code **11%**

(8,798) Equipment **13%**

0.3% Phishing (194)

0.1% Denial of Service (85)

25% Non Cyber (16,879)

19% Scans/Probes/ Attempted Access (12,652)

17% Policy Violation (11,588)

Source: GAO analysis of United States Computer Emergency Readiness Team data for fiscal year 2014. | GAO-15-758T

These incidents and others like them can adversely affect national security; damage public health and safety; and lead to inappropriate access to and disclosure, modification, or destruction of sensitive information. Recent examples highlight the impact of such incidents:

- In June 2015, OPM reported that an intrusion into its systems affected personnel records of about 4 million current and former federal employees. The Director of OPM also stated that a separate incident may have compromised OPM systems related to background investigations, but its scope and impact have not yet been determined.

- In June 2015, the Commissioner of the Internal Revenue Service (IRS) testified that unauthorized third parties had gained access to taxpayer information from its "Get Transcript" application. According to IRS, criminals used taxpayer-specific data acquired from non-IRS sources to gain unauthorized access to information on approximately 100,000 tax accounts. These data included Social Security information, dates of birth, and street addresses.

62

- In April 2015, the Department of Veterans Affairs (VA) Office of Inspector General reported that two VA contractors had improperly accessed the VA network from foreign countries using personally owned equipment.

- In February 2015, the Director of National Intelligence stated that unauthorized computer intrusions were detected in 2014 on OPM's networks and those of two of its contractors. The two contractors were involved in processing sensitive PII related to national security clearances for federal employees.

- In September 2014, a cyber-intrusion into the United States Postal Service's information systems may have compromised PII for more than 800,000 of its employees.

Federal Agencies Face Ongoing Cybersecurity Challenges

Given the risks posed by cyber threats and the increasing number of incidents, it is crucial that federal agencies take appropriate steps to secure their systems and information. We and agency inspectors general have identified challenges in protecting federal information and systems, including those in the following key areas:

- **Designing and implementing risk-based cybersecurity programs at federal agencies.** Agencies continue to have shortcomings in assessing risks, developing and implementing security controls, and monitoring results. Specifically, for fiscal year 2014, 19 of the 24 federal agencies covered by the Chief Financial Officers (CFO) Act[5] reported that information security control deficiencies were either a material weakness or a significant deficiency in internal controls over

[5]The 24 agencies are the Departments of Agriculture, Commerce, Defense, Education, Energy, Health and Human Services, Homeland Security, Housing and Urban Development, the Interior, Justice, Labor, State, Transportation, the Treasury, and Veterans Affairs; the Environmental Protection Agency; General Services Administration; National Aeronautics and Space Administration; National Science Foundation; Nuclear Regulatory Commission; Office of Personnel Management; Small Business Administration; Social Security Administration; and the U.S. Agency for International Development.

their financial reporting.[6] Moreover, inspectors general at 23 of the 24 agencies cited information security as a major management challenge for their agency.

As we testified in April 2015, for fiscal year 2014, most of the agencies had weaknesses in the five key security control categories.[7] These control categories are (1) limiting, preventing, and detecting inappropriate access to computer resources; (2) managing the configuration of software and hardware; (3) segregating duties to ensure that a single individual does not have control over all key aspects of a computer-related operation; (4) planning for continuity of operations in the event of a disaster or disruption; and (5) implementing agency-wide security management programs that are critical to identifying control deficiencies, resolving problems, and managing risks on an ongoing basis. (See fig. 3.)

---

[6]A material weakness is a deficiency, or combination of deficiencies, that results in more than a remote likelihood that a material misstatement of the financial statements will not be prevented or detected. A significant deficiency is a control deficiency, or combination of control deficiencies, in internal control that is less severe than a material weakness, yet important enough to merit attention by those charged with governance. A control deficiency exists when the design or operation of a control does not allow management or employees, in the normal course of performing their assigned functions, to prevent or detect and correct misstatements on a timely basis.

[7]GAO, Cybersecurity: Actions Needed to Address Challenges Facing Federal Systems, GAO-15-573T (Washington, D.C.: Apr. 22, 2015).

Figure 3: Information Security Weaknesses at 24 Federal Agencies for Fiscal Year 2014

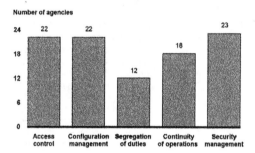

Source: GAO analysis of agencies, Inspector General and GAO reports as of April 17, 2015. | GAO-15-758T

Examples of these weaknesses include: (1) granting users access permissions that exceed the level required to perform their legitimate job-related functions; (2) not ensuring that only authorized users can access an agency's systems; (3) not using encryption to protect sensitive data from being intercepted and compromised; (4) not updating software with the current versions and latest security patches to protect against known vulnerabilities; and (5) not ensuring employees were trained commensurate with their responsibilities. We and agency inspectors general have made hundreds of recommendations to agencies aimed at improving their implementation of these information security controls.

- **Enhancing oversight of contractors providing IT services.** In August 2014, we reported that five of six agencies we reviewed were inconsistent in overseeing assessments of contractors' implementation of security controls.[8] This was partly because agencies had not documented IT security procedures for effectively overseeing contractor performance. In addition, according to OMB, 16 of 24 agency inspectors general determined that their agency's program for managing contractor systems lacked at least one required element. We recommended that the reviewed agencies establish and

---

[8]GAO, *Information Security: Agencies Need to Improve Oversight of Contractor Controls,* GAO-14-612 (Washington, D.C.: Aug. 8, 2014).

implement IT security oversight procedures for such systems. The agencies generally concurred with our recommendations. We also made one recommendation to OPM and the agency concurred, but has not yet implemented this recommendation.

- **Improving security incident response activities.** In April 2014, we reported that the 24 agencies did not consistently demonstrate that they had effectively responded to cyber incidents.[9] Specifically, we estimated that agencies had not completely documented actions taken in response to detected incidents reported in fiscal year 2012 in about 65 percent of cases.[10] In addition, the 6 agencies we reviewed had not fully developed comprehensive policies, plans, and procedures to guide their incident response activities. We recommended that OMB address agency incident response practices government-wide and that the 6 agencies improve the effectiveness of their cyber incident response programs. The agencies generally agreed with these recommendations.

- **Responding to breaches of PII.** In December 2013, we reported that eight federal agencies had inconsistently implemented policies and procedures for responding to data breaches involving PII.[11] In addition, OMB requirements for reporting PII-related data breaches were not always feasible or necessary. Thus, we concluded that agencies may not be consistently taking actions to limit the risk to individuals from PII-related data breaches and may be expending resources to meet OMB reporting requirements that provide little value. We recommended that OMB revise its guidance to agencies on responding to a PII-related data breach and that the reviewed agencies take specific actions to improve their response to PII-related data breaches. OMB neither agreed nor disagreed with our recommendation; four of the reviewed agencies agreed, two partially agreed, and two neither agreed nor disagreed.

- **Implementing security programs at small agencies.** In June 2014, we reported that six small agencies (i.e., agencies with 6,000 or fewer

---

[9]GAO, *Information Security: Agencies Need to Improve Cyber Incident Response Practices*, GAO-14-354 (Washington, D.C.: Apr. 30, 2014).

[10]This estimate was based on a statistical sample of cyber incidents reported in fiscal year 2012, with 95 percent confidence that the estimate falls between 58 and 72 percent.

[11]GAO, *Information Security: Agency Responses to Breaches of Personally Identifiable Information Need to Be More Consistent*, GAO-14-34 (Washington, D.C.: Dec. 9, 2013).

employees) had not implemented or not fully implemented their information security programs.[12] For example, key elements of their plans, policies, and procedures were outdated, incomplete, or did not exist, and two of the agencies had not developed an information security program with the required elements. We recommended that OMB include a list of agencies that did not report on the implementation of their information security programs in its annual report to Congress on compliance with the requirements of FISMA, and include information on small agencies' programs. OMB generally concurred with our recommendations. We also recommended that DHS develop guidance and services targeted at small agencies. DHS agreed and has implemented this recommendation.

Until federal agencies take actions to address these challenges—including implementing the hundreds of recommendations we and inspectors general have made—federal systems and information will be at an increased risk of compromise from cyber-based attacks and other threats.

Government-wide Cybersecurity Initiatives Present Potential Benefits and Challenges

In addition to the efforts of individual agencies, DHS and OMB have several initiatives under way to enhance cybersecurity across the federal government. While these initiatives all have potential benefits, they also have limitations.

Personal Identity Verification: In August 2004, Homeland Security Presidential Directive 12 ordered the establishment of a mandatory, government-wide standard for secure and reliable forms of identification for federal government employees and contractor personnel who access government-controlled facilities and information systems. Subsequently, NIST defined requirements for such personal identity verification (PIV) credentials based on "smart cards"—plastic cards with integrated circuit chips to store and process data—and OMB directed federal agencies to issue and use PIV credentials to control access to federal facilities and systems.

In September 2011, we reported that OMB and the eight agencies in our review had made mixed progress for using PIV credentials for controlling

---

[12]GAO, *Information Security: Additional Oversight Needed to Improve Programs at Small Agencies*, GAO-14-344 (Washington, D.C.: June 25, 2014).

access to federal facilities and information systems.[13] We attributed this mixed progress to a number of obstacles, including logistical problems in issuing PIV credentials to all agency personnel and agencies not making this effort a priority. We made several recommendations to the eight agencies and to OMB to more fully implement PIV card capabilities. Although two agencies did not comment, seven agencies agreed with our recommendations or discussed actions they were taking to address them. For example, we made four recommendations to DHS. The department concurred and has taken action to implement them.

In February 2015, OMB reported that, as of the end of fiscal year 2014, only 41 percent of agency user accounts at the 23 civilian CFO Act agencies required PIV cards for accessing agency systems.[14] At OPM, only 1 percent of user accounts required PIV cards for such access.

Continuous Diagnostics and Mitigation (CDM): According to DHS, this program is intended to provide federal departments and agencies with capabilities and tools that identify cybersecurity risks on an ongoing basis, prioritize these risks based on potential impacts, and enable cybersecurity personnel to mitigate the most significant problems first. These tools include sensors that perform automated searches for known cyber vulnerabilities, the results of which feed into a dashboard that alerts network managers. These alerts can be prioritized, enabling agencies to allocate resources based on risk. DHS, in partnership with the General Services Administration, has established a government-wide contract that is intended to allow federal agencies (as well as state, local, and tribal governmental agencies) to acquire CDM tools at discounted rates.

In July 2011, we reported on the Department of State's (State) implementation of its continuous monitoring program, referred to as iPost.[15] We determined that State's implementation of iPost had improved

---

[13]GAO, *Personal ID Verification: Agencies Should Set a Higher Priority on Using the Capabilities of Standardized Identification Cards*, GAO-11-751 (Washington, D.C.: Sept. 20, 2011).

[14]OMB, *Annual Report to Congress: Federal Information Security Management Act* (Washington, D.C.: Feb. 27, 2015).

[15]GAO, *Information Security: State Has Taken Steps to Implement a Continuous Monitoring Application, but Key Challenges Remain*, GAO-11-149 (Washington, D.C.: July 8, 2011)

visibility over information security at the department and helped IT administrators identify, monitor, and mitigate information security weaknesses. However, we also noted limitations and challenges with State's approach, including ensuring that its risk-scoring program identified relevant risks and that iPost data were timely, complete, and accurate. We made several recommendations to improve the implementation of the iPost program, and State partially agreed.

National Cybersecurity Protection System (NCPS): The National Cybersecurity Protection System, operationally known as "EINSTEIN," is a suite of capabilities intended to detect and prevent malicious network traffic from entering and exiting federal civilian government networks. The EINSTEIN capabilities of NCPS are described in table 3.[16]

Table 3: National Cybersecurity Protection System EINSTEIN Capabilities

Operational name	Capability intended	Description
EINSTEIN 1	Network Flow	Provides an automated process for collecting, correlating, and analyzing agencies' computer network traffic information from sensors installed at their Internet connections.[a]
EINSTEIN 2	Intrusion Detection	Monitors federal agency Internet connections for specific predefined signatures of known malicious activity and alerts US-CERT when specific network activity matching the predetermined signatures is detected.[b]
EINSTEIN 3 Accelerated	Intrusion Prevention	Automatically blocks malicious traffic from entering or leaving federal civilian executive branch agency networks. This capability is managed by Internet service providers, who administer intrusion prevention and threat-based decision-making using DHS-developed indicators of malicious cyber activity to develop signatures.[c]

Source: GAO analysis of DHS documentation and prior GAO reports. | GAO-15-758T

[a]The network traffic information includes source and destination Internet Protocol addresses used in the communication, source and destination ports, the time the communication occurred, and the protocol used to communicate.

[b]Signatures are recognizable, distinguishing patterns associated with cyber attacks, such as a binary string associated with a computer virus or a particular set of keystrokes used to gain unauthorized access to a system.

[c]An indicator is defined by DHS as human-readable cyber data used to identify some form of malicious cyber activity. These data may be related to Internet Protocol addresses, domains, e-mail headers, files, and character strings. Indicators can be either classified or unclassified.

In March 2010, we reported that while agencies that participated in EINSTEIN 1 improved their identification of incidents and mitigation of attacks, DHS lacked performance measures to understand if the initiative

---

[16]In addition to the EINSTEIN capabilities listed in table 1, NCPS also includes a set of capabilities related to analytics and information sharing.

was meeting its objectives.[17] We made four recommendations regarding the management of the EINSTEIN program, and DHS has since taken action to address them.

Currently, we are reviewing NCPS as directed by Senate and House reports accompanying the Consolidated Appropriations Act, 2014. The objectives of our review are to determine the extent to which (1) NCPS meets stated objectives, (2) DHS has designed requirements for future stages of the system, and (3) federal agencies have adopted the system.

Our final report is expected to be released later this year, and our preliminary observations include the following:

- DHS appears to have developed and deployed aspects of the intrusion detection and intrusion prevention capabilities, but potential weaknesses may limit their ability to detect and prevent computer intrusions. For example, NCPS detects signature anomalies using only one of three detection methodologies identified by NIST: signature-based, anomaly-based, and stateful protocol analysis. Further, the system has the ability to prevent intrusions, but is currently only able to proactively mitigate threats across a limited subset of network traffic (i.e., Domain Name System traffic and e-mail).

- DHS has identified a set of NCPS capabilities that are planned to be implemented in fiscal year 2016, but it does not appear to have developed formalized requirements for capabilities planned through fiscal year 2018.

- The NCPS intrusion detection capability appears to have been implemented at 23 CFO Act agencies.[18] The intrusion prevention capability appears to have limited deployment at portions of only 5 of these agencies. Deployment may have been hampered by various implementation and policy challenges.

In conclusion, the danger posed by the wide array of cyber threats facing the nation is heightened by weaknesses in the federal government's approach to protecting its systems and information. While recent

---

[17]GAO, *Information Security: Concerted Effort Needed to Consolidate and Secure Internet Connections at Federal Agencies*, GAO-10-237 (Washington, D.C.: Mar. 12, 2010).

[18]The Department of Defense is not required to implement EINSTEIN.

government-wide initiatives hold promise for bolstering the federal cybersecurity posture, it is important to note that no single technology or set of practices is sufficient to protect against all these threats. A "defense in depth" strategy is required that includes well-trained personnel, effective and consistently applied processes, and appropriately implemented technologies. While agencies have elements of such a strategy in place, more needs to be done to fully implement it and to address existing weaknesses. In particular, implementing GAO and inspector general recommendations will strengthen agencies' ability to protect their systems and information, reducing the risk of a potentially devastating cyber attack.

Chairwoman Comstock, Chairman Loudermilk, Ranking Members Lipinski and Beyer, and Members of the Subcommittees, this concludes my statement. I would be happy to answer your questions.

Contact and Acknowledgments

If you have any questions about this statement, please contact Gregory C. Wilshusen at (202) 512-6244 or wilshuseng@gao.gov. Other staff members who contributed to this statement include Larry Crosland and Michael Gilmore (assistant directors), Bradley Becker, Christopher Businsky, Nancy Glover, Rosanna Guerrero, Kush Malhotra, and Lee McCracken.

71

Related GAO Products

Cybersecurity: Recent Data Breaches Illustrate Need for Strong Controls across Federal Agencies. GAO-15-725T. June, 24, 2015.

Cybersecurity: Actions Needed to Address Challenges Facing Federal Systems. GAO-15-573T. April 22, 2015.

Information Security: IRS Needs to Continue Improving Controls over Financial and Taxpayer Data. GAO-15-337. March 19, 2015.

Information Security: FAA Needs to Address Weaknesses in Air Traffic Control Systems. GAO-15-221. January 29, 2015.

Information Security: Additional Actions Needed to Address Vulnerabilities That Put VA Data at Risk. GAO-15-220T. November 18, 2014.

Information Security: VA Needs to Address Identified Vulnerabilities. GAO-15-117. November 13, 2014.

Federal Facility Cybersecurity: DHS and GSA Should Address Cyber Risk to Building and Access Control Systems. GAO-15-6. December 12, 2014.

Consumer Financial Protection Bureau: Some Privacy and Security Procedures for Data Collections Should Continue Being Enhanced. GAO-14-758. September 22, 2014.

Healthcare.Gov: Information Security and Privacy Controls Should Be Enhanced to Address Weaknesses. GAO-14-871T. September 18, 2014.

Healthcare.Gov: Actions Needed to Address Weaknesses in Information Security and Privacy Controls. GAO-14-730. September 16, 2014.

Information Security: Agencies Need to Improve Oversight of Contractor Controls. GAO-14-612. August 8, 2014.

Information Security: FDIC Made Progress in Securing Key Financial Systems, but Weaknesses Remain. GAO-14-674. July 17, 2014.

Information Security: Additional Oversight Needed to Improve Programs at Small Agencies. GAO-14-344. June 25, 2014.

Maritime Critical Infrastructure Protection: DHS Needs to Better Address Port Cybersecurity. GAO-14-459. June 5, 2014.

72

Information Security: Agencies Need to Improve Cyber Incident Response Practices. GAO-14-354. April 30, 2014.

Information Security: SEC Needs to Improve Controls over Financial Systems and Data. GAO-14-419. April 17, 2014.

Information Security: IRS Needs to Address Control Weaknesses That Place Financial and Taxpayer Data at Risk. GAO-14-405. April 8, 2014.

Information Security: Federal Agencies Need to Enhance Responses to Data Breaches. GAO-14-487T. April 2, 2014.

Critical Infrastructure Protection: Observations on Key Factors in DHS's Implementation of Its Partnership Model. GAO-14-464T. March 26, 2014.

Information Security: VA Needs to Address Long-Standing Challenges. GAO-14-469T. March 25, 2014.

Critical Infrastructure Protection: More Comprehensive Planning Would Enhance the Cybersecurity of Public Safety Entities' Emerging Technology. GAO-14-125. January 28, 2014.

Computer Matching Act: OMB and Selected Agencies Need to Ensure Consistent Implementation. GAO-14-44. January 13, 2014.

Information Security: Agency Responses to Breaches of Personally Identifiable Information Need to Be More Consistent. GAO-14-34. December 9, 2013.

Federal Information Security: Mixed Progress in Implementing Program Components; Improved Metrics Needed to Measure Effectiveness. GAO-13-776. September 26, 2013.

Communications Networks: Outcome-Based Measures Would Assist DHS in Assessing Effectiveness of Cybersecurity Efforts. GAO-13-275. April 10, 2013.

Information Security: IRS Has Improved Controls but Needs to Resolve Weaknesses. GAO-13-350. March 15, 2013.

Cybersecurity: A Better Defined and Implemented National Strategy is Needed to Address Persistent Challenges. GAO-13-462T. March 7, 2013.

73

Cybersecurity: National Strategy, Roles, and Responsibilities Need to Be Better Defined and More Effectively Implemented. GAO-13-187. February 14, 2013.

Information Security: Federal Communications Commission Needs to Strengthen Controls over Enhanced Secured Network Project. GAO-13-155. January 25, 2013.

Information Security: Actions Needed by Census Bureau to Address Weaknesses. GAO-13-63. January 22, 2013.

Information Security: Better Implementation of Controls for Mobile Devices Should Be Encouraged. GAO-12-757. September 18, 2012.

Mobile Device Location Data: Additional Federal Actions Could Help Protect Consumer Privacy. GAO-12-903. September 11, 2012.

Medical Devices: FDA Should Expand Its Consideration of Information Security for Certain Types of Devices. GAO-12-816. August 31, 2012.

Privacy: Federal Law Should Be Updated to Address Changing Technology Landscape. GAO-12-961T. July 31, 2012.

Information Security: Environmental Protection Agency Needs to Resolve Weaknesses. GAO-12-696. July 19, 2012.

Cybersecurity: Challenges in Securing the Electricity Grid. GAO-12-926T. July 17, 2012.

Electronic Warfare: DOD Actions Needed to Strengthen Management and Oversight. GAO-12-479. July 9, 2012.

Information Security: Cyber Threats Facilitate Ability to Commit Economic Espionage. GAO-12-876T. June 28, 2012.

Prescription Drug Data: HHS Has Issued Health Privacy and Security Regulations but Needs to Improve Guidance and Oversight. GAO-12-605. June 22, 2012.

Cybersecurity: Threats Impacting the Nation. GAO-12-666T. April 24, 2012.

74

Management Report: Improvements Needed in SEC's Internal Control and Accounting Procedure. GAO-12-424R. April 13, 2012.

IT Supply Chain: National Security-Related Agencies Need to Better Address Risks. GAO-12-361. March 23, 2012.

Information Security: IRS Needs to Further Enhance Internal Control over Financial Reporting and Taxpayer Data. GAO-12-393. March 16, 2012.

Cybersecurity: Challenges in Securing the Modernized Electricity Grid. GAO-12-507T. February 28, 2012.

Critical Infrastructure Protection: Cybersecurity Guidance is Available, but More Can Be Done to Promote Its Use. GAO-12-92. December 9, 2011.

Cybersecurity Human Capital: Initiatives Need Better Planning and Coordination. GAO-12-8. November 29, 2011.

Information Security: Additional Guidance Needed to Address Cloud Computing Concerns. GAO-12-130T. October 6, 2011.

76

GAO's Mission	The Government Accountability Office, the audit, evaluation, and investigative arm of Congress, exists to support Congress in meeting its constitutional responsibilities and to help improve the performance and accountability of the federal government for the American people. GAO examines the use of public funds; evaluates federal programs and policies; and provides analyses, recommendations, and other assistance to help Congress make informed oversight, policy, and funding decisions. GAO's commitment to good government is reflected in its core values of accountability, integrity, and reliability.
Obtaining Copies of GAO Reports and Testimony	The fastest and easiest way to obtain copies of GAO documents at no cost is through GAO's website (http://www.gao.gov). Each weekday afternoon, GAO posts on its website newly released reports, testimony, and correspondence. To have GAO e-mail you a list of newly posted products, go to http://www.gao.gov and select "E-mail Updates."
Order by Phone	The price of each GAO publication reflects GAO's actual cost of production and distribution and depends on the number of pages in the publication and whether the publication is printed in color or black and white. Pricing and ordering information is posted on GAO's website, http://www.gao.gov/ordering.htm. Place orders by calling (202) 512-6000, toll free (866) 801-7077, or TDD (202) 512-2537. Orders may be paid for using American Express, Discover Card, MasterCard, Visa, check, or money order. Call for additional information.
Connect with GAO	Connect with GAO on Facebook, Flickr, Twitter, and YouTube. Subscribe to our RSS Feeds or E-mail Updates. Listen to our Podcasts. Visit GAO on the web at www.gao.gov.
To Report Fraud, Waste, and Abuse in Federal Programs	Contact: Website: http://www.gao.gov/fraudnet/fraudnet.htm E-mail: fraudnet@gao.gov Automated answering system: (800) 424-5454 or (202) 512-7470
Congressional Relations	Katherine Siggerud, Managing Director, siggerudk@gao.gov, (202) 512-4400, U.S. Government Accountability Office, 441 G Street NW, Room 7125, Washington, DC 20548
Public Affairs	Chuck Young, Managing Director, youngc1@gao.gov, (202) 512-4800 U.S. Government Accountability Office, 441 G Street NW, Room 7149 Washington, DC 20548

Please Print on Recycled Paper.

77

Biography

Gregory Wilshusen is Director of Information Security Issues at GAO, where he leads cybersecurity and privacy-related studies and audits of the federal government and critical infrastructure. He has over 30 years of auditing, financial management, and information systems experience. Prior to joining GAO in 1997, Mr. Wilshusen held a variety of public and private sector positions. He was a senior systems analyst at the Department of Education. He also served as the Controller for the North Carolina Department of Environment, Health, and Natural Resources, and held senior auditing positions at Irving Burton Associates, Inc. and the U.S. Army Audit Agency. He's a certified public accountant, certified internal auditor, and certified information systems auditor. He holds a B.S. degree in business administration (accounting) from the University of Missouri and an M.S. in information management from George Washington University's School of Engineering and Applied Sciences.

78

Chairwoman COMSTOCK. I thank the witnesses for their testimony and for your expertise and work on this over quite a long time.

I would like to remind Members that the Committee rules limit our questioning to five minutes and I now recognize myself for five minutes of questions.

A Washington Post editorial from this past Sunday, July 5, they said the OPM Director knew as well as anyone how sensitive the data was, yet the door to her agency was apparently left ajar. Thieves walked out with an intelligence goldmine. This was an unforgivable failure of stewardship that should lead to firings for incompetence.

Mr. Esser, to your knowledge has OPM reprimanded or fired any official over this failure to protect its employees' most sensitive data?

Mr. ESSER. I'm not aware of any.

Chairwoman COMSTOCK. Are you aware of any discussions to that effect?

Mr. ESSER. No, I haven't heard any.

Chairwoman COMSTOCK. Okay. Thank you.

And, Mr. Snell, really thank you for being here and representing so many people not just here in our metropolitan area but all across the country because this impacts our contractors, our federal employees, so it's important for people to understand that this is really a nationwide breach and, you know, you're representing people who are aware of this but there's still many more that aren't. Could you tell us what some of their concerns and unanswered questions are and how you think additional things that might be helpful for the employees and from what you've heard that we might ask for to help answer the questions that you've been getting from people?

Mr. SNELL. Thank you. I'd be glad to. A lot of the folks we hear from are members as well as others. Their main concern is trust and trust in what they get. The information came to many of them through email. The email address was not a government email address. It was a .com address. They didn't know whether to open it, they didn't know what to do with it. They had little information. Many people have received letters. Those people don't have internet. They didn't—they weren't able to access the frequently asked questions and the explanations that the Office of Personnel Management had available out there. And so they were left in the dark.

They didn't know if they called the number, if they contacted anybody if they could ever trust them, so we have a lot of distrust out there. A lot of folks are scared obviously. They don't know what's going happen. Some folks who have not been notified that their records were compromised are wondering, you know, were my records compromised? Can I trust the fact that I didn't get notice or is this another, you know, problem? So those are the questions, those are the concerns that we hear from our members both current federal employees and retirees.

Chairwoman COMSTOCK. Thank you. I appreciate that and we look forward to continuing to work with you on identifying any of those and how we can help answer their questions.

I was wondering, maybe a question for all of you, what kind of things, if someone has had their information breached or compromised, what should they be on the lookout for now? What would be an unusual type of situation that should raise the antenna and say this might be something I need to pay attention to? Can you think of some scenarios just so that people can get an idea of what they have to be on the lookout for?

Dr. WILSHUSEN. Sure. I'll start it off. First of all, individuals who believe their information may have been compromised or been notified that it has been should certainly check their credit reports to see if there have been any new credit accounts or charges that they're unaware of that may have cropped up, and certainly that's probably one of the basic things that individuals should do. They should also know that they are entitled to receive a free credit report from each of the three credit reporting agencies on an annual basis and that's something that one should do on a regular basis annually is to check each—credit reports from each of those organizations.

Indeed, if they do receive the letter, as I have, is to also check to see about subscribing to the service that OPM is offering through their contractor because they, too, will provide—or supposed to provide anyway—some surveillance on the part of the individual.

Chairwoman COMSTOCK. Okay.

Mr. SNELL. I would add to that—and those are excellent suggestions. I would add to that that any statement they get regarding any other benefits they get from any other company or government entity such as Social Security, if there's something that has changed without their knowledge, they should report that right away. We had one member who found out his address on his Social Security payments had changed without his authorization. Being this close to the events of the breaches, of course, that member was concerned that this had been connected. But we did report it to OPM. The OPM folks had looked into it and decided that it was a separate incident. But still, any kind of changes like that, people should look into.

Chairwoman COMSTOCK. Okay. And one other thing I was wondering, should—a lot of people don't know what's necessarily in their personnel file. Have people asked you about possibly having copies of their personnel file, having copies of their background check? Because, you know, if something starts coming up, you don't necessarily know what's in your background check, right, or even your personnel file even though you fill it out. Particularly with the background checks, those people aren't going to have any idea what people have said, right?

Mr. SNELL. Right. We haven't heard from anybody—any of our members with that particular request so—

Chairwoman COMSTOCK. Okay. Thank you. And I now turn over to questions from Mr. Lipinski.

Mr. LIPINSKI. Thank you. I want to get down to the big question and what—in terms of what we should do moving forward here. It's not acceptable for these data breaches to occur at OPM, anywhere else in the government, or in the private sector. We know—okay, we accept—we know that they can happen but I sometimes feel like there's not enough done not just in the public sector but the private sector to prevent these.

So my question is how do we make FISMA effective? I understand, as Dr. Romine said, that NIST, for good reason, only sets the standards; they're not the enforcer. So who should be, who can be the enforcer when it comes to the federal government? And I want to—just want to try to figure this out so that we can get someone so we know who's accountable, who can be held accountable, and who has the responsibility. So, Mr. Esser, what would you recommend?

Mr. ESSER. Well, one possibility is OMB. I mean we—as an IG office we audit, we report, and we identify, you know, areas of weakness but that's as far as our authority extends. We have no enforcement authority. Those reports go eventually to OMB and that could potentially be one area of enforcement.

Mr. LIPINSKI. Dr. Romine, do you have any recommendations?

Dr. ROMINE. No, I think that's right. The oversight function, as it currently is set up under FISMA, I think is OMB with more recently DHS providing assistance to agencies to meet their obligations under FISMA. So I think that's the right answer.

Mr. LIPINSKI. Mr. Wilshusen, do you have anything to add?

Dr. WILSHUSEN. Yeah, I would agree to same extent that both of the other witnesses mentioned, but I would also just like to point out that under the FISMA 2002 and FISMA 2014 it is clearly the responsibility of the head of each agency to implement the appropriate information security protections to reduce the risk and magnitude of harm that could occur should information or information systems be compromised through unauthorized access, use, disclosure, modification, destruction, and disruption. And so clearly in terms of responsibility it's the head of agencies—each agency head to make that happen.

Mr. LIPINSKI. Is there anything more that you recommend that we do? As you said, FISMA has been updated but is there anything more that should be done with, you know, that Congress should do with FISMA? Does anyone have any recommendations for anything further?

Dr. WILSHUSEN. Well, I would just say first that I think Congress did—went quite a distance in terms of modernizing FISMA to include clarifying their roles and responsibilities for information security across the federal government, particularly with assigning responsibilities to the Department of Homeland Security, who has now responsibility for assisting and overseeing to an extent implementation security controls at the federal agencies.

It also recognizes the need for new types of security controls and procedures to be put in place such as continuous monitoring, continuous diagnostics and mitigation, which is another type of control set that, if effectively implemented, could assist agencies in better protecting their systems, identifying their risk, and addressing the key vulnerabilities first.

Mr. LIPINSKI. Okay. Mr. Esser, did you want to add something?

Mr. ESSER. Yeah. I agree with Mr. Wilshusen, and I think from our viewpoint, the FISMA Modernization Act of 2014 went a long ways toward improving the situation, changing our reviews from more of a compliance check of a yes or a no, do they have—or do they do security controls testing to an effectiveness test of how good are those tests and moving towards continuous monitoring and the mature model that is being put in place. So we think continuing to move along that path is the right direction.

Mr. LIPINSKI. Anyone else have anything to add?

Good. All right. Thank you very much. I yield back.

Chairwoman COMSTOCK. Thank you.

And I now recognize Mr. Loudermilk.

Mr. LOUDERMILK. Thank you, Madam Chair.

Mr. Wilshusen, as I mentioned in my opening statement, the situation we have at OPM is exactly why my subcommittee is investigating the collection of America's personal data through HealthCare.gov. In September 2014, the GAO came out with a report noting that HealthCare.gov's data warehouse system MIDAS did not have an approved Privacy Impact Assessment that included a thorough analysis of privacy risks. Given that MIDAS is processing personally identifiable information and appears to have—indefinitely storing that information, how important is it to have an approved privacy impact statement for—or assessment for MIDAS?

Dr. WILSHUSEN. I think it's vitally important because in that it helps the agencies to identify not only the privacy risks associated with that particular system but also alternatives and the controls that should be in place to better protect and help protect that information.

Mr. LOUDERMILK. Thank you.

Dr. WILSHUSEN. And we recommended—we also noted that not only had CMS not effectively implemented—or designed a policy impact assessment for MIDAS but for other systems connected with HealthCare.gov.

Mr. LOUDERMILK. Do you know if an assessment is done since the September report?

Dr. WILSHUSEN. We just received information from—we actually made a recommendation that in their Privacy Impact Assessment that they assess these privacy risks and today we believe that recommendation is still open——

Mr. LOUDERMILK. So do they——

Dr. WILSHUSEN. —and not fully implemented by——

Mr. LOUDERMILK. They have not—is that concerning?

Dr. WILSHUSEN. Well, we believe they should do that, yes.

Mr. LOUDERMILK. Okay. When you looked into the MIDAS system as part of the HealthCare.gov review, was it known to you that personally identifiable information of individuals who signed up on the HealthCare.gov website would be indefinitely stored?

Dr. WILSHUSEN. It was known that initially the CMS officials indicated that personally identifiable information may not be stored and it—but then they acknowledged that it would be and it was because of that acknowledgement that personally identifiable information would be stored in MIDAS, that the need for assessing those privacy risks is important as part of a Privacy Impact Assessment.

Mr. LOUDERMILK. Okay. So the fact that they indicated that they intended to store this PII information is really what catapulted this assessment, the need for the assessment? Is that what you're saying?

Dr. WILSHUSEN. Right. Any new development or system should have a Privacy Impact Assessment if personally identifiable information is going to be collected, stored, or disseminated through that system.

Mr. LOUDERMILK. Is it normal for the federal government to store PII information on websites or information obtained through websites?

Dr. WILSHUSEN. I would say that that is normal for agencies to store personally identifiable information, some of which may be obtained through a website, but we—I have not looked at that specifically with regard to collection of information through websites.

Mr. LOUDERMILK. Okay. I appreciate that. Also, GAO has listed the security of our federal cyber assets on its high-risk list since 1997. It's been almost 20 years. Does it remain on the high-risk list to this day because of evolving threats to federal information systems or is it because federal agencies have not been able to learn how to properly protect these systems?

Dr. WILSHUSEN. I would say both——

Mr. LOUDERMILK. Okay.

Dr. WILSHUSEN. —because certainly there's an inherent risk to agency systems because of the evolving threats and just the complexity of the systems that agencies develop and operate because many—much of the software that agencies use have vulnerabilities in it, some discovered, some undiscovered. But at the same time it's incumbent upon federal agencies to implement the appropriate security controls to mitigate those risks to—at a cost-effective and acceptable level. And we found that agencies have not consistently implemented agencywide information security programs to mitigate that risk effectively.

Mr. LOUDERMILK. Is it because of—it's a lack of priority for a lot of these agencies?

Dr. WILSHUSEN. In some cases it might be but it's also in other cases I believe it's just to the fact that there are a number of actions that agencies just haven't really taken that they need to take such as installing patches on a timely manner and assuring that known vulnerabilities are ameliorated in a timely manner.

Mr. LOUDERMILK. Can you tell me who's ultimately accountable for the cybersecurity of our federal government?

Dr. WILSHUSEN. Accountable or responsible? You know, I have to say in terms of at least for federal agencies, the agency head is responsible for implementing effective security controls and that's under law under FISMA. At the same time in terms of accountable that's harder to measure because to my knowledge it's difficult to see what accountability mechanisms are in place to assure that individuals are effectively securing systems. That could be done through personnel performance expectations, but in terms of individuals being held to account for that is somewhat uncertain.

Mr. LOUDERMILK. I see I'm out of time. One quick question if I may, Madam Chair.

Chairwoman COMSTOCK. We're just tight because we're going to have votes.

Mr. LOUDERMILK. Okay.

Chairwoman COMSTOCK. We want to squeeze everybody in.

Mr. LOUDERMILK. On a scale grading like elementary school A to F, our federal cybersecurity, how do you grade it?

Dr. WILSHUSEN. D.

Mr. LOUDERMILK. D minus from the way I hear that?

Dr. WILSHUSEN. I'll go with D because in many respects there are improvements within federal information security and some of the initiatives but it's getting to the effective implementation of those security controls and the—some of the initiatives. Over time, consistently, that's been proved challenging.

Mr. LOUDERMILK. Thank you very much. Thanks to all the panel.

Chairwoman COMSTOCK. Thank you.

I now recognize Mr. Beyer for five minutes.

Mr. BEYER. Thank you, Madam Chair.

Mr. Snell, do you know how long it takes to have a negative report, a so-called derogatory report on your credit report drop off?

Mr. SNELL. [Nonverbal response.]

Mr. BEYER. Okay. Well, six to eight years. I only bring that up because it's a long time.

Mr. SNELL. It is a long time.

Mr. BEYER. And I want to bring—call attention to something that you mentioned in your written report where you say "the federal government should offer identity theft insurance, should offer credit monitoring services for the lifetime of anyone affected, and increase the amount of identity theft insurance provided in certain circumstances. Unlimited coverage may be required." I just want all of us to highlight that because this is I think really an initiative that we can bring as Democrats and as Republicans on Oversight to this issue.

Mr. SNELL. Well, thank you.

Mr. BEYER. So thank you for bringing that up because it—by the way, the other rhetorical question, do you know how long it takes them to fix something that's wrong on a credit report, which is like impossible? So——

Mr. SNELL. It's a nightmare.

Mr. BEYER. Yes.

Mr. Esser, your testimony was pretty devastating, all the things that didn't get fix that were identified year in and year out within OPM. And I'm just baffled by it. Do you have any idea why? Is this a series of CIOs who didn't respond? Is it a series of Directors, Democrat, Republican administrations that didn't respond? Does any of it come back to us on Congress because we didn't allocate the resources necessary, the hardware, the software, the staffing to make all this happen? For example, you mentioned in there that OPM has decided they needed a legacy system. With legacy systems, you couldn't go back and tinker with them one by one; you had to do an overhaul. Help us understand this lack of leadership and lack of action on something that you guys as Inspectors General had clearly identified.

Mr. ESSER. I would have to guess it's a combination of factors. Certainly, there's been, you know, different directors and different CIOs during the time period that we've reported material weaknesses in IT security. You know, so, you know, if you look at the current Director, she wasn't there when this all started. The current CIO wasn't there when this all started. But at the same time

84

there's been current issues that we've reported that, you know, they also haven't gotten addressed in a timely fashion that we would like to see them addressed.

Resources I think is always an issue but it's not the sole answer. I think sometimes we feel like things that we report don't get the attention that they should get. We've had, you know, weaknesses that have been outstanding for, you know, years and years and years and that just shouldn't be.

Mr. BEYER. All right. Well, thank you. Thank you, Mr. Esser.

Dr. Romine, did I say that right?

Dr. ROMINE. [Nonverbal response.]

Mr. BEYER. On NPR this morning they were talking about the difficulty that our military and our intelligence units are having with ISIS encrypting messages between their potential recruits. Can we use this encryption for federal government data?

Dr. ROMINE. I don't know what encryption they're using but we do have access to strong encryption, and in fact NIST in my laboratory has been in the encryption space for decades now starting with the original DES, Data Encryption Standard, that was developed through NIST.

We certainly recognized—our guidance provides input that encryption is a very powerful tool for securing information. It's not the only one in the arsenal but it is a very effective one and often not very costly. And so I think certainly it's an avenue for protecting the data.

Mr. BEYER. You know, I know you're not responsible for the private sector and it seems that you clearly have developed some very thoughtful guidelines and protocols for how the federal government should work. Do you have any sense of whether the federal government leads or lags the private sector in terms of cybersecurity, data encryption, all the things we're talking about today?

Dr. ROMINE. So I think there are bright spots in both cases. I mean I think there are—it's uneven in the private sector just as it's uneven in the federal government as well. I will say that the guidelines and the standards that we issue that are principally intended for the federal government are often picked up by the private sector because of the quality of those guidelines and standards. And in fact we depend on the private sector to participate and provide us with input. We have a multiphase comment period for almost all of our guidelines so that we get the best minds in the private sector and public sector to contribute.

Mr. BEYER. Thank you.

Madam Chair, I yield back.

Chairwoman COMSTOCK. Thank you.

I now recognize Mr. Johnson for five minutes.

Mr. JOHNSON. Thank you, Madam Chairman. And, gentlemen, thank you for joining us today.

I—you know, cybersecurity and the kind of attack that we saw on OPM I think—and I believe I read it here somewhere earlier today—is just the tip of the iceberg. As a 30-year IT professional myself, I firmly understand that as long as computers are working off of 1s and 0s, the bad guys are going to be out there trying to get in. And the battle space is huge and our ability to protect it is going to require constant vigilance. It's not a problem that has—

it's not a race that has a finish line because as soon as we get to one point, the goalposts are moved and the game strategy changes.

And I spent a lot of my time helping to educate and inform those that will listen so that we understand. But this is a big issue and communications and computing technologies are foundational to our economy and to virtually every industry that supports our economy, including our own national security. So it's a really big issue.

Mr. Esser, the OPM Director has stated that some of OPM's network systems are so old that it has been difficult if not impossible to upgrade and encrypt them. How credible is that explanation and how many of the OPM systems that were hacked were these old legacy systems versus more modern ones capable of encryptions and upgrades?

Mr. ESSER. I don't have an exact count of how many are legacy systems and how many are modern. There is a lot of credibility to what she says. There are old systems at OPM that it is difficult to bring into the modern area of security, not that it can't be done but it can be difficult. But our understanding is that at least a few of the systems that were hacked are more modern systems that certainly, you know, modern encryption techniques and other security techniques could have been implemented on.

Mr. JOHNSON. Right. Okay. Well, a complete overhaul of the existing IT infrastructure at OPM could take years, right? Do you believe that there are intermediate steps OPM could take to address security needs in the short-term?

Mr. ESSER. There are and they have taken some of those steps. They've—

Mr. JOHNSON. What are those? Can you enumerate some of them?

Mr. ESSER. Well, when the initial breach took place in 2014 and they began working on tightening up their systems, they went into what they call a tactical phase of immediately remediating some of the high security problems they had. And so we're fully in favor of everything they've done related that. You know, things like, you know, requiring more two-factor authentication. They're not fully there but they're working on it so they have taken steps to tighten up systems in that respect.

Mr. JOHNSON. Okay. Dr. Romine and Mr. Wilshusen—do I have that right?

Dr. WILSHUSEN. Close enough. It's Wilshusen.

Mr. JOHNSON. Wilshusen, okay. I apologize. Johnson is pretty easy for everybody so I don't ever have that problem. Sorry.

Dr. Romine and Mr. Wilshusen, do you agree? Are there things that can be done in the near term? Are there more things that can be done in the near term?

Dr. ROMINE. Well, certainly from the perspective of the NIST guidelines and FISMA guidelines that we issue I think we put those out as a means of reducing the susceptibility of the system to hack. Nothing is 100 percent secure but I think following those guidelines is the most effective way that I can think of to protect the systems.

Mr. JOHNSON. Mr. Wilshusen?

Dr. WILSHUSEN. And I would agree with both what Dr. Romine and Mr. Esser said. One thing that comes to mind, too, is based on what's been reported by the Office of Management and Budget as it relates to OPM is that, as of the end of fiscal year 2014, OPM had only implemented the use of personal identity verification cards or strong authentication for one percent of its user accounts. My understanding is that they're making progress now to improve that but certainly having strong authentication, using multifactor authentication for user accounts would be one area that it seems that OPM could improve on and may be working on that now.

Mr. JOHNSON. Okay. Well, gentlemen, thank you very much and I've exhausted my time.

Madam Chair, I yield back.

Chairwoman COMSTOCK. Thank you.

I now recognize Ms. Bonamici.

Ms. BONAMICI. Thank you very much, Madam Chair. Thanks to the Chairs and Ranking Members for this important conversation and thanks to the witnesses who are here. I wish we each had five hours instead of five minutes because there are so many questions.

So I wanted to start, Mr. Snell, you mentioned the issues and the challenges with notification and communication, and this is something that I want to recognize both in the public and private sector has been a challenge. And of course with the number of current and former federal employees, it's my understanding that the FISMA requirement requires notice to affected individuals provided as expeditiously as practicable and without unreasonable delay. So those are obviously terms that are not concrete depending on the circumstances. I just bring this up to recognize the importance of communicating with people who are victims of the data breaches. And it's not just an issue in the federal arena either, in the private sector as well.

I want to go back to the point that was made about encryption. It's my understanding that Estonia, even though it's a small country, had a significant data breach in 2007 and has really come around and is now considered one of the countries that does the best job of protecting data. Granted it's a smaller—much smaller population but they do make—heavy use of encryption. And they also have focused on educating the workforce.

And I also serve on the Education Committee and I wanted to ask about the—whether we are really educating people who will be able to be the people who are preventing as well as understanding how we need to do this both psychologically and technically. So do we need to improve cybersecurity education? Are there enough opportunities for the workforce? Do we have the people we need out there to be able to do these jobs? I'll start with Mr. Wilshusen.

Dr. WILSHUSEN. Well, I think certainly improving the cybersecurity understanding and awareness on the part of the public at large, which I believe you're referring to, as well as with the federal workforce, is going to be very important to address these cyber threats that consistently evolve and are becoming more sophisticated over time. And certainly having an awareness of that and what types of controls and activities one should engage in and should not engage in should be certainly on the minds and—of everyone because each individual potentially could be the weak link in—which results in some sort of a computer compromise.

Ms. BONAMICI. That's a great point. And in your testimony you have this whole chart about the common adversaries and you list hackers and I have to say I'm a little confused as I go visit schools and the high schools are having these hack-a-thons and they're considered positive things. So is hacker a negative connotation or is it a positive or is it—depends on who the hacker is? It's a little confusing.

Dr. WILSHUSEN. I guess it depends on what they're doing with their hacking. You know, if they're so-called white hackers, you know, but in terms of—it's good to know how hackers and particularly those individuals with malicious intent——

Ms. BONAMICI. Right.

Dr. WILSHUSEN. —operate, what types of tools they use, how—their modus operandi if you will in order to understand how to protect against them. And so it's important to know that and certainly one of the things that information security professionals do is penetration testing and to see whether or not any organization's information security controls are effective in keeping out hackers who may use similar type of techniques.

Ms. BONAMICI. Terrific. And I wanted to ask, I guess, each of you. Can you talk a little bit about your—what are your two or three top recommendations for improving practices generally, not necessarily just for the federal government. Mr. Esser, what would be your top two or three recommendations?

Mr. ESSER. I mean one of the things I would go back to is the two-factor authentication to strengthen security. It's really necessary to implement that and not just that but I mean there's all kinds of different things that need to be implemented, and the key I think is having, you know, security Defense in Depth I think is the term that's used.

Ms. BONAMICI. Terrific. And I want to make sure the others get—and I'm almost out of time.

Mr. Snell, do you have a couple of——

Mr. SNELL. No, that's not my strength so I'll——

Ms. BONAMICI. Dr. Romine?

Dr. ROMINE. Sure. I would echo, I think, that proper identity management is a key driver. I think it can be really beneficial. Good use of encryption is good for preserving the integrity or at least the confidentiality of data, so I would just maybe add those two.

Ms. BONAMICI. And Mr. Wilshusen?

Dr. WILSHUSEN. I would say one is addressing patches or installing critical patches and remediating known vulnerabilities. U.S. CERT recently came out with a technical alert that said if you address these top 30 targeted vulnerabilities, that would address up to 85 percent of the targeted vulnerabilities that are currently being used. The other thing would be improved detection and prevention capabilities because regardless of how well you protect your systems, it's likely you still may be subject to attack from unknown vulnerabilities.

Ms. BONAMICI. Thank you so much. I see my time is expired. I yield back. Thank you.

Chairwoman COMSTOCK. Thank you. And I would just take privilege to note, I know when I was visiting schools that also do the hacking and training them, you know, that—it's a great growth area for kids to get engaged in and get educated on because there's going to be lots of jobs for them in this area. And I know somebody who works in the business so they tell their clients if we can't hack into your system, you shouldn't hire us to protect your system because that's part of what their job is to constantly be looking for the next attack, right? So that's—thank you.

I now recognize Mr. Abraham for five minutes.

Dr. ABRAHAM. Thank you, Madam Chair.

I guess first I'll express my disappointment for the Chief Information Officer Ms. Seymour not—or declining our invitation to come speak here. It's my understanding that she has extensive involvement in preparing this system. Might I suggest that if OPM had put extensive involvement in preventing this, we might not even be having this hearing. So just that as a statement.

Mr. Wilshusen, I'm going to start with you. Has the federal government's response to this breach in your opinion been sufficient?

Dr. WILSHUSEN. Well, one of the responses—and I can't necessarily speak specifically to OPM, but more broadly speaking, as you may know, the federal CIO issued an initiative or a proclamation known as the 30-day Cybersecurity Sprint, and indeed, you know, to the extent that that 30-day sprint raises awareness and invigorates activity towards addressing these basic security requirements included in the sprint such as installing critical patches, assuring deploying multifactor authentication, and other—resolving known vulnerabilities, that's important. And to the extent that that gets done, that's a positive.

But where it may become detrimental if after this 30 days, which expires on Sunday, by the way, that the agencies and the federal government relaxes and thinks, okay, we've accomplished our goal, I think that's a mistake because cybersecurity and implementing effective security is not a sprint; it's a marathon. And it's something that needs to be going on a continuous basis. And the fact of just going back to—possibly going back to the status quo, which only led to the conditions that resulted in the need for a 30-day sprint.

So I would say it raised awareness. Agencies may be taking actions to improve their security, but that needs to continue in perpetuity.

Dr. ABRAHAM. And I'll follow up with you, Mr. Wilshusen. Knowing what you know about the cybersecurity or lack thereof of all our federal agencies, would you entrust any of your sensitive information with any of these agencies?

Dr. WILSHUSEN. In some cases I have no choice because my information is at other agencies through security clearances and the like and through our tax systems and issuing tax returns, and so, yes, I do entrust personal information to agencies and that's why it's important and incumbent upon those agencies to adequately protect information that the American taxpayers, the American public entrust to it.

Dr. ABRAHAM. And it's my understanding that the GAO tracks the history of these breaches. How does this OPM recent breach compare or where does it rank in the history of the other government breaches as far as the tracking is concerned?

Dr. WILSHUSEN. Well, in terms of the like number of individuals affected by this breach—

Dr. ABRAHAM. Right.

Dr. WILSHUSEN. —it's among the top. You know, a few years ago back I think in 2005, 2006 there was a data breach at the Department of Veterans Affairs in which the hard drive was stolen from an employee's—from their home but that contained the personally identifiable information of 26, 27 million veterans and current service members. But that hard drive was ultimately found and determined not to have been—the information was determined not to have been disclosed. So that—this particular breach ranks right up near the top I would say.

Dr. ABRAHAM. Mr. Esser, you said in your testimony that the OPM leadership has been—has not been forthright about the claim of proactively shutting down the e-QIP system. Can you tell us how long the OPM has known about these vulnerabilities to that particular one system?

Mr. ESSER. There was a security assessment and authorization done on the e-QIP system in September of 2012 which identified 18 vulnerabilities. I do not know if those vulnerabilities are related to the reason that the system was shut down last week but it certainly indicates that there has been vulnerabilities that OPM has been aware of and has not addressed even to date.

Dr. ABRAHAM. Okay. Thank you.

Madam Chair, I'll yield back.

Chairwoman COMSTOCK. Thank you, Mr. Abraham.

Ms. Esty.

Ms. ESTY. Thank you, Madam Chair. I want to thank you and Chairman Loudermilk and Ranking Members Lipinski and Beyer for holding today's extremely important hearing. And as we've—as has already been noted, with three other breaches having been noted today in the private sector, it's very much on all of our minds.

Our national and personal security depends on a strong cybersecurity infrastructure, and the recent breaches that have been disclosed with OPM are to me particularly disturbing when I look at the security clearance records that could have been compromised. No credit check is going to make up for the risk to not just personal security but our nation's security for every individual who went through or was consulted as part of that system.

So I'd like you to think and maybe get back to us on what sort of protection and advice do we give on the national security front, on the security breach aspect because that is very different than your personal information to raid your bank account. That's a risk of grave concern for this country, which we haven't really discussed today.

It seems to me a number of issues have been raised and I want to quickly tick them off and then focus on the last. We need to understand the extent of vulnerability and that's been discussed at some length. The accountability for what's happened also been raised by other Members. And I want to focus on the last two, our capacity to address these issues in the future. That's a question in part of resources and that's been mentioned, both personnel resources—and Representative Bonamici raised an issue she and I share a grave concern and interest in, encouraging young people to pursue these fields and making sure we have enough capacity on both the private sector side and the public sector side. Is it a priority issue? Do we need to have different prioritization?

But the last issue I'd really like you to respond to is how do we move to a continuous monitoring or effectiveness model from what we've had, which is a compliance model? It seems to me we have a real challenge. Congress enacts laws. Laws are about compliance. They are snapshots in time that reflect our knowledge and technical capabilities. But as we've all discussed here today, these are evolving risks, and the moment we stick a pin in the butterfly and pin it down, it will change by the time we finish pushing that pin in.

So if you could discuss a little bit what can we do on the Congressional side and what can the agencies due to move to a mindset that is much more nimble and that is in a continuous mode because that's going to be both what our hard and software look like but also our mindset about what compliance actually means.

Dr. WILSHUSEN. I'll take first stab if you don't mind.

Well, one is an initiative that's already underway within the Department of Homeland Security as it relates to continuous diagnostics and mitigation, the extent to which DHS is providing tools that are available for agencies to implement this capability. Our work at the Department of State before this initiative was established showed that there are benefits to monitoring the security posture of an organization on a continuous basis, but there are also a number of challenges associated with that, some technological, some management and operational.

But certainly that's one area that can be done and indeed Congress in the passage of the Federal Information Security Modernization Act of 2014 recognized the need for continuous monitoring and identified that as one of the areas that agencies should be focusing on in securing their systems. And so that's one part of it.

But you're right, I totally agree. The need for assessing and monitoring the effectiveness of security controls needs to be done on a continuous monitoring basis because threats change every day, the computing environment changes is very dynamic, and new vulnerabilities are being identified each time.

Dr. ROMINE. If I may, I'd like to spotlight two things that NIST is doing that address two of your issues. One is we house the program office for the National Initiative for Cybersecurity Education, which is an interagency activity that I think is making great strides in addressing the workforce issue that you brought up.

And the second is under Executive Order 13636 NIST engaged the private sector and other stakeholders in a year-long effort to develop what turned into the cybersecurity framework for improving the cybersecurity of critical infrastructures. And although that was the focus, it has turned out that that report that we developed the framework is a model I think for establishing or improving a cybersecurity approach whether it's in the private sector or the public sector or other areas. It's a very dynamic approach that involves, you know, a development of maturity along the lines of—analogous to a maturity model and so I think that could be really beneficial.

Chairwoman COMSTOCK. Okay. Thank you.

Ms. ESTY. I see my time is expired.

Chairwoman COMSTOCK. We want to be able to squeeze in our last two folks here.

Mr. Palmer, I recognize you for five minutes.

Mr. PALMER. Thank you, Madam Chairman.

We've talked about Defense in Depth and the hardware but I want to talk about the individuals involved.

Dr. Wilshusen, OPM and the Department of Homeland Security officials stated that the attackers who reached OPM's systems may have been aided by user credentials that were obtained or stolen from one of OPM's contractors. Andy Ozment testified before the Oversight Committee that part of this breach may have occurred through social engineering. I want to know in your opinion what agencies can do to ensure that their IT contractors are effectively protecting federal systems and information? I mean I fully get it that we need to completely overhaul our hardware and software, but that alone in the context of Defense in Depth will not secure the system.

Dr. WILSHUSEN. I wholeheartedly agree. The oversight of contractors and their information security practices over systems that they operate on behalf of the federal government or operate to process information on behalf of the federal government is really critical to assure that—agencies need to assure that that information is being adequately protected. And that requires that they go in and assess or have an independent assessor evaluate the security controls and assure that they're being operated effectively and efficiently and that indeed the requirements for information security are expressed to the contractor either through contractual instruments or other mechanisms to assure that they know what is required to help protect those systems.

And another point you raised in terms of—was the stolen user credentials that might have been used to help promote or facilitate the attack on OPM, one of the things that could help there is having multifactor authentication, which would help to either prevent or at least raise the bar significantly for that attacker to be able to use compromised credentials. And that wasn't in place in all places throughout OPM.

Mr. PALMER. Well, it's even worse than that. Dr. Ozment—it wasn't in his testimony but in an interview—talked about the fact that one of the contractors working with OPM was based in Argentina and was working with two people who were Republic of China nationals. I mean how do we let something like that happen? I mean with the amount of cyber assault—I visited a facility that monitors these cyber attacks and you can literally see them being launched. There were 700 and something cyber attacks launched from Russia with 10 minutes. China was a distant second.

How is it that we would not be aware that we had people foreign-based involved in this and particularly a couple of Chinese nationals?

Dr. WILSHUSEN. I guess I'm not familiar with that particular situation so I don't know if I can really comment to that, so——

Mr. PALMER. But I think you would agree, though, that that's a pretty egregious oversight or failure to exercise oversight over our systems?

Dr. WILSHUSEN. I think it's important that agencies understand who has access to their systems and are accessing their systems and that kind of gets back to the identity management area that we—the panel spoke about earlier. So that certainly is one specific point to that.

Mr. PALMER. Mr. Snell, I want to ask you something here. Mr. Abraham brought up the fact that Ms. Seymour did not want to testify before this committee. When she testified before the Oversight Committee, I asked her if the breach was limited only to people who filled out the Standard Form 86, the security background check, because that was I think the position that OPM had taken. It turns out that it extends beyond that. Two of my staff who have never filled out an SF 86, who have never served in the executive branch, both got letters telling them that their personal data had been compromised.

Do you have an idea of how broad this is and does it extend beyond current federal employees to retired employees? Is it possible that it would extend to civilians who have national security clearances?

Mr. SNELL. That's entirely possible. We don't have firsthand information. We only know what's being reported out of OPM and it's not very much. It's not very helpful what they're reporting as far as numbers but it's entirely—and it has been I think in the media mentioned that it could be contractors, as well as federal employees, former employees, people who are no longer in the federal government. So I'd have to turn that back over to the Office of Personnel Management to come forth with information letting us know exactly who the victims of these breaches are.

Mr. PALMER. Madam Chairman, I yield the balance of my time. Thank you.

Chairwoman COMSTOCK. Thank you.

And I now recognize five minutes for Mr. Tonko.

Mr. TONKO. Thank you, Madam Chair.

The—being a former federal employee, Mr. Snell, what are the kinds of communication that you would like to see happen?

Mr. SNELL. Well, in a situation like this I would like to see the communication be sent via letter with OPM agency seal on it so that the individuals would be able to at least feel confident that this is an official U.S. Government notice. And that kind of—I know it's not efficient in today's email world and all of that, but in a case like this where we have the credibility issue as to who do you trust, who do you don't trust, I think a letterhead—OPM letterhead or an agency letterhead would have gone a lot further to helping folks believe what they're getting is bona fide. So I like that like that kind of communication.

Mr. TONKO. Thank you.

And Mr. Esser, the review here that was done would obviously involve the private sector, right, with contractors serving the federal government with some of the reinforcement here? How—was there any review done of that private sector element?

Mr. ESSER. I'm not sure I understand what review you're referring to.

Mr. TONKO. Well, just with the outcome that we had in the situation, were contractors reviewed in this situation that served the federal agencies?

Mr. ESSER. I'm sorry. I guess I still don't quite understand the question. What review are you referring to?

Mr. TONKO. Just the malfunctioning that occurred. As we look over the situation and try to determine where the weaknesses in the system are, what—is there a role that the contractors to the system might have played here or that could have been better collaboration involved in this system? Were there any recommendations that you could make in that regard?

Mr. ESSER. If—I mean we in the IG office, when we do our reviews, certainly there's contractor-operated systems at OPM and we look at those the same way we look at the agency-operated systems. I mean there's a number of contractors that are working at OPM and likely at many other agencies as well. They, I believe, are treated the same way as federal employees in how we conduct our reviews.

Mr. TONKO. And in those reviews was there a need for better collaboration in this whole process where there could have been perhaps a stronger partnership with those efforts?

Mr. ESSER. I don't believe we reported any issues in that area.

Mr. TONKO. And to any of you on the panel, when we look at a situation like this, is there a concern for the amount of available resources to an agency to prevent any of this activity? Is it a function of lack of resources or how those resources have been shared? Would any of you comment on, you know, weak investment or falling short in the resources we require?

Dr. WILSHUSEN. You know, broadly speaking, not just talking to OPM but across the federal government, many of the security control deficiencies and weaknesses that we identified during our audits are more of an information security management process more than a lack of resources in terms of implementing effectively and consistently across an agency its own defined and developed policies and procedures.

For example, one basic control is just installing patches on a timely manner, particularly those that have been rated as critical. Agencies often have policies that state they need to be installed within a certain period of time, usually within a week or a couple weeks, but we find that sometimes those patches are not being installed for months and sometimes over years. So, in part it's a management issue to make sure that these key security control issues and controls are being effectively implemented.

There are also resource implications as well. In some cases it may be important for agencies to implement new technologies or tools, particularly with respect to installing intrusion detection capabilities within their networks to identify those types of vulnerabilities or cyber attacks or intrusions that do inevitably occur.

Mr. TONKO. Thank you very much. I see my time is out. Thank you, Madam Chair.

Chairwoman COMSTOCK. Thank you. And we do have a vote now and so I just want to thank the witnesses for their very valuable testimony today. Sorry we had to sandwich it in between our votes because I know myself and my colleagues could spend a lot more time talking with you about this and will be talking with you and asking for any guidance that you can give us with your expertise. So we very much appreciate you coming before us.

The record will remain open for two weeks for additional comments and written questions from the Members.

And so the witnesses are excused and we thank you again for your expert testimony. And this hearing is adjourned.

[Whereupon, at 5:19 p.m., the Subcommittees were adjourned.]

Appendix I

ANSWERS TO POST-HEARING QUESTIONS

Responses by Mr. Michael R. Esser
HOUSE COMMITTEE ON SCIENCE, SPACE, AND TECHNOLOGY
SUBCOMMITTEE ON RESEARCH AND TECHNOLOGY
SUBCOMMITTEE ON OVERSIGHT

"Is the OPM Data Breach the Tip of the Iceberg?"

Mr. Michael R. Esser, Assistant Inspector General for Audits, Office of Personnel Management

Questions submitted by Rep. Barbara Comstock, Chairwoman, Subcommittee on Research and Technology and Rep. Barry Loudermilk, Chairman, Subcommittee on Oversight

1. In previous congressional testimony, you stated that the U.S. Office of Personnel Management (OPM) Chief Information Officer (CIO) has temporarily put authorizations of its systems security on hold while it modernizes OPM's IT infrastructure in response to the breaches. You have recommended that the Authorization process should continue.

    a. How has OPM responded to that recommendation?

    OPM OIG Response: *We have not yet documented this recommendation in any formal correspondence, and therefore OPM has not provided us with a response. We continue to believe that OPM should continue subjecting all of its information systems to the Authorization process. A thorough evaluation of OPM's Authorization process is part of our annual FISMA audit, which is underway now. We anticipate issuing a draft report that addresses this issue in September 2015.*

    b. In part you stated that you made that recommendation because modernization is likely to be a long term effort. Does your office have an estimate for how much time it will take OPM to modernize its systems to meet compliance with FISMA standards?

    OPM OIG Response: *We have no way of knowing how long it will take OPM to modernize its systems. One of our primary concerns is that OPM still has not completed an inventory of the systems that need to be modernized, and therefore it is not possible for anyone to provide a reasonable estimate of the timeline.*

2. In your written testimony you stated that the OPM Office of the Chief Information Officer instituted restructuring changes in 2014, to better centralize information security, including the establishment of a 24/7 security operations center. However, your testimony also stated that "OPM has not yet implemented a mature continuous monitoring program."

a. Can you explain why a continuous monitoring program is important?

OPM OIG Response: Federal cybersecurity has historically been assessed by periodic point-in-time assessments of IT security controls. Information system owners were required to perform "self-assessments" of their system's controls on an annual basis, and each system was required to be subjected to a thorough independent assessment of security controls every three years (i.e., the Authorization process). In today's dynamic IT environment, these periodic assessments are not sufficient. In order to better detect and prevent security breaches, all information systems need to be monitored on a near real-time basis using automated tools to increase efficiency.

b. Why do you believe OPM has failed to implement such a program?

OPM OIG Response: OPM's struggle to implement a mature continuous monitoring program is largely the result of its decentralized and fragmented network architecture. As mentioned above, continuous monitoring programs rely on the use of automated tools. While OPM has personnel staffed in its security operations center 24/7 and does have some of these tools available, they cannot be fully effective if they cannot reach all of the agency's information systems. For example, our Fiscal Year 2014 FISMA report noted that although OPM uses an automated security information and event management (SIEM) tool to analyze security incidents throughout the network, this tool receives data from only 80 percent of OPM's major information systems.

We have also reported that OPM does not have a well-defined inventory of all of its IT assets. Automated continuous monitoring tools cannot be effective unless they cover the entire environment – a task that is not possible without a well-defined inventory. Until OPM has implemented a mature continuous monitoring program, we expect the agency to continue performing routine point-in-time assessments of IT security controls (the Authorization process). While this process is labor intensive, more expensive, and less efficient than continuous monitoring, it is a critical step in identifying IT security weaknesses so that they can be remediated - thereby significantly reducing the risk of data breaches.

3. How does OPM store individuals' fingerprints for background investigations and did the OPM Office of the Inspector General find any vulnerability in OPM's process for storing them or make any recommendations regarding that process. If so, what were they and what was OPM's response to those recommendations?

OPM OIG Response: Individuals' fingerprints are managed by an OPM system called the Fingerprint Transaction System. The details of how OPM stores fingerprints could be more accurately provided by the agency. We have not reported any vulnerabilities related to this process.

4. Was there a backup or archive of the stolen data – in other words, does OPM still have any of the stolen data, or is it gone so that the perpetrators have it and the United States no longer does?

    OPM OIG Response: *This question should be directed to OPM.*

5. After taking it offline for a brief period, OPM has restored online access to the EQIP (Electronic Questionnaires for Investigations Processing) system. Has the OIG been consulted in the interim and are you satisfied that OPM has appropriately fixed the security vulnerability it discovered?

OPM OIG Response: *OPM did consult with us regarding the e-QIP security vulnerabilities and provided us a detailed description of the additional controls it implemented to make the system more secure. We are satisfied that these additional controls reduced the security risks to a level acceptable to bring the system back online, but note that a long-term effort is required to rebuild the system in a more secure*

HOUSE COMMITTEE ON SCIENCE, SPACE, AND TECHNOLOGY
SUBCOMMITTEE ON RESEARCH AND TECHNOLOGY
SUBCOMMITTEE ON OVERSIGHT

"Is the OPM Data Breach the Tip of the Iceberg?"

Mr. Michael R. Esser, Assistant Inspector General for Audits, Office of Personnel Management

Questions submitted by Rep. Elizabeth Esty, Member, Subcommittee on Research and Technology

1. The day after the hearing, the U.S. Office of Personnel Management (OPM) announced
   the results of the investigation into the recent cyber-attack that involved the Federal
   background investigation data. The investigation found that the security clearance
   background information of 21.5 million individuals was compromised. Along with
   including significant information about the individual (Social Security Numbers, current
   and former addresses, education background, current and former employment
   information, financial information, travel information, mental health information,
   criminal background and substance use), the security clearance background information
   form includes information about the individual's friends and relatives and foreign
   contacts as well. Due to the extensive information included on the security clearance
   background forms, I am concerned that standard credit monitoring its insufficient
   protection. Please describe the kinds of protections that are needed to help protect
   individuals who were compromised in this breach.

   *OPM OIG Response: The Federal Bureau of Investigation and the U.S. Computer
   Emergency Readiness Team are the entities leading the investigation into the breach. It
   is our understanding that the investigation, which is still ongoing, will involve an
   analysis of the impact of the breach on individuals. Until that analysis is complete, it is
   difficult to determine what measures would be sufficient to protect the victims from future
   harm.*

100

Responses by Mr. David Snell

HOUSE COMMITTEE ON SCIENCE, SPACE, AND TECHNOLOGY
SUBCOMMITTEE ON RESEARCH AND TECHNOLOGY
SUBCOMMITTEE ON OVERSIGHT

"Is the OPM Data Breach the Tip of the Iceberg?"

Mr. David Snell, Director, Federal Benefits Service Department, National Active and Retired Federal Employee Association

Questions submitted by Rep. Elizabeth Esty, Member, Subcommittee on Research and Technology

1. The day after the hearing, the Office of Personnel Management (OPM) announced the results of the investigation into the recent cyber-attack that involved the Federal background investigation data. The investigation found that the security clearance background information of 21.5 million individuals was compromised. Along with including significant information about the individual (Social Security Numbers, current and former addresses, education background, current and former employment information, financial information, travel information, mental health information, criminal background, and substance use), the security clearance background information form includes information about the individual's friends and relatives and foreign contacts as well. Due to the extensive information included on the security clearance background forms, I am concerned that standard credit monitoring is insufficient protection. Please describe the kinds of protections that are needed to help protect individuals who were compromised in this breach.

Response to Question for the Record by Rep. Elizabeth Esty, Member, Subcommittee on Research and Technology

NARFE supports the following **lifetime** protections for those individuals whose personally-identifiable information was compromised:

- Identity theft insurance.
- Credit monitoring.
- Identity monitoring for minor children.
- Full identity restoration support and victim recovery assistance.
- Fraud monitoring services beyond credit files.

These protections should be provided to individuals affected by both the security clearance background information data breach, and the civilian federal employee personnel file data breach.

The security clearance background information breach made available a treasure-trove of sensitive personal information – beyond basic personally-identifiable information, such as Social Security number and date of birth. This sensitive personal information could give our enemies the means to attempt to corrupt or blackmail government employees and compromise military and intelligence secrets. Moreover, it could lead to the possibility that particular public servants would become vulnerable to grave risks that could threaten their personal security and that of their families and loved ones.

Unfortunately, it is difficult to put this genie back in the bottle, and there is not an easy solution to protecting against these more personal threats. Yet we must do everything within our capacity to prevent them from harming our national security and the personal security of those individuals with whom we entrust it. We look forward to working with policymakers in both the executive and legislative branches towards this end.

HOUSE COMMITTEE ON SCIENCE, SPACE, AND TECHNOLOGY
SUBCOMMITTEE ON RESEARCH AND TECHNOLOGY
SUBCOMMITTEE ON OVERSIGHT

"Is the OPM Data Breach the Tip of the Iceberg?"

Mr. Gregory Wilshusen, Director, Information Security Issues, U.S. Government Accountability Office

Questions submitted by Rep. Barbara Comstock, Chairwoman, Subcommittee on Research and Technology
and Rep. Barry Loudermilk, Chairman, Subcommittee on Oversight

1. **The Federal CIO recently announced a "30-day Cybersecurity Sprint" to enhance and strengthen the federal government's cybersecurity. Is this an effective approach to cybersecurity?**

    To the extent that the 30-day cybersecurity sprint increases awareness of the need to better protect federal information systems and invigorates agency efforts to implement basic security requirements, it is a positive step. In June 2015, the Federal CIO announced the 30-day sprint and directed agencies to immediately patch critical vulnerabilities, review and tightly limit the number of privileged users with access to authorized systems, and dramatically accelerate the use of strong authentication.[1] In a July 31, 2015 blog posting, the Federal CIO announced that agencies made significant progress in implementing the use of strong authentication during the sprint.[2]

    However, effectively securing an agency's information systems and networks is more a marathon than a sprint. The actions required by the sprint are fundamental cybersecurity practices that agencies had already been required to perform and for which we have consistently identified weaknesses during our audits of agency information security programs. That the sprint focused attention on implementing these practices is beneficial. But it may become detrimental if agencies relax now that the sprint is over, and return to their previous modus operandi, which led to the weakened security environment.

    A more effective approach for strengthening federal information security is to implement a "defense-in-depth" strategy that incorporates multiple layers of security controls and includes top management support, pertinent policies, effective and disciplined processes, well-trained personnel, appropriate technologies, and consistent oversight to sustain effective information security on an ongoing basis.

---

[1] OMB, FACT SHEET: Enhancing and Strengthening the Federal Government's Cybersecurity (Washington, D.C.: June 12, 2015).

[2] https://www.whitehouse.gov/blog/2015/07/31/strengthening-enhancing-federal-cybersecurity-21st-century

2. You testified that GAO has identified federal information security as a government-wide high risk area since 1997. Why is it taking the government so long to address this problem?

Several factors complicate federal efforts to effectively secure its information systems. First, cyber threats to federal systems are evolving, growing, and becoming more sophisticated. Adversaries such as criminal groups, hackers, disgruntled employees, and foreign nations are prevalent, agile, and increasingly skilled in perpetrating targeted cyberattacks. They vary in terms of their capabilities, willingness to act, and motives, which can include seeking monetary gain or pursuing a political, economic, or military advantage. For example, adversaries possessing sophisticated levels of expertise and significant resources to pursue their objectives—sometimes referred to as "advanced persistent threats"—pose increasing risks. These adversaries make use of various techniques, tactics, and practices or "exploits" to adversely affect federal information, computers, software, networks, and operations, which further complicates federal efforts to thwart them.

Second, federal systems are inherently vulnerable to cyber threats. Federal computing environments are often large, complex, and dynamic. They consist of a variety of information and communications technologies, operating and application software, computer and networking equipment, data storage and portable devices. The complexity and diversity of these environments makes them challenging to manage, maintain, and secure. The software supporting federal systems is often riddled with security deficiencies and defects. For example, the national vulnerability database maintained by the National Institute of Standards and Technology has identified over 70,000 software defects and misconfigurations that could place the software at risk, with 19 more being added each day on average. Federal systems are also increasingly interconnected to other systems and internal and external networks in order to deliver services and perform mission-essential functions and operations. This increased interconnectivity can increase the number of access paths that an intruder may exploit.

Third, federal agencies have been challenged in effectively designing and implementing risk-based cybersecurity programs. As I have previously testified, [3] for fiscal year 2014, 19 of the 24 federal agencies covered by the Chief Financial Officers (CFO) Act reported that information security control deficiencies were either a material weakness or a significant deficiency in internal control for financial reporting purposes.[4] In addition, most agencies had weaknesses in five key control categories.[5] For example, 22 of the 24

---

[3] GAO, *Cybersecurity: Actions Needed to Address Challenges Facing Federal Systems*, GAO-15-573T (Washington, D.C. Apr. 22, 2015).

[4] A material weakness is a deficiency, or combination of deficiencies, that results in more than a remote likelihood that a material misstatement of the financial statements will not be prevented or detected. A significant deficiency is a control deficiency, or a combination of control deficiencies, in internal control that is less severe than a material weakness, yet important enough to merit attention by those charged with governance. A control deficiency exists when the design or operation of a control does not allow management or employees, in the normal course of performing their assigned functions, to prevent or detect and correct misstatements on a timely basis.

[5] These categories include controls that are intended to 1) limit, detect, and prevent unauthorized access to computer resources; 2) manage the configuration of software and hardware; 3) segregate incompatible duties to ensure that a

CFO Act agencies had weaknesses with limiting, preventing, and detecting inappropriate access to computer resources, and managing the configuration of software and hardware. Agencies have also been challenged in overseeing the information security controls of their contractors providing IT services, responding to cyber incidents and responding to breaches of personally identifiable information. Moreover, the Inspectors General at 23 of the 24 agencies cited information security as a major management challenge for their agency.

3. **You have authored a number of reports at GAO about cybersecurity deficiencies across the federal government. What are the next potential hacks, or known cybersecurity vulnerabilities, that the Committee should be concerned about?**

While one cannot predict the future with certainty, I believe our adversaries will continue to target federal agencies and their contractors with the intent to gain unauthorized access to federal systems and the sensitive information they contain. The adversaries will also likely continue to target private sector companies and the owners and operators of our nation's critical infrastructure. To facilitate their schemes, malicious actors will likely use phishing and spear phishing exploits to trick individuals into providing information or downloading malicious software to gain entrée to the agency's or organization's network. Intruders will likely use zero day exploits or exploit unpatched software and poorly configured systems to expand their access and achieve their objectives.

Regarding known cybersecurity vulnerabilities, the U.S. Computer Emergency Readiness Team (US-CERT) recently issued a technical alert (TA15-119A) that identified the top 30 targeted high-risk vulnerabilities as of April 2015.[6] These vulnerabilities affect systems running unpatched software from Adobe, Microsoft, Oracle, or OpenSSL. Unpatched vulnerabilities allow malicious actors entry points into a network. According to the alert, up to 85 percent of targeted attacks are preventable.

In its oversight role, the committee may wish to consider how well federal agencies are implementing steps to mitigate these vulnerabilities, such as maintaining up-to-date software, patching commonly exploited vulnerabilities, and restricting administrative privileges.

---

single individual does not have control over all key aspects of a computer-related operation; 4) planning for continuity of operations in the event of a disaster or disruption; and 5) implementing agency-wide security management programs that are critical to identifying control deficiencies, resolving problems, and managing risks on an ongoing basis.

[6] https://www.us-cert.gov/ncas/alerts/TA15-119A

HOUSE COMMITTEE ON SCIENCE, SPACE, AND TECHNOLOGY
SUBCOMMITTEE ON RESEARCH AND TECHNOLOGY
SUBCOMMITTEE ON OVERSIGHT

"Is the OPM Data Breach the Tip of the Iceberg?"

Mr. Gregory Wilshusen, Director, Information Security Issues, U.S. Government Accountability Office

Questions submitted by Rep. Elizabeth Esty, Member, Subcommittee on Research and Technology

1. **The day after the hearing, the Office of Personnel Management (OPM) announced the results of the investigation into the recent cyber-attack that involved the Federal background investigation data. The investigation found that the security clearance background information of 21.5 million individuals was compromised. Along with including significant information about the individual (Social Security Numbers, current and former addresses, education background, current and former employment information, financial information, travel information, mental health information, criminal background, and substance use), the security clearance background information form includes information about the individual's friends, relatives, and foreign contacts as well. Due to the extensive information included in the security clearance background forms, I am concerned that standard credit monitoring is insufficient protection. Please describe the kinds of protections that are needed to help protect individuals who were compromised in this breach.**

In addition to credit report and monitoring, the following protections are available to individuals whose information has been compromised by the OPM cyber-attack:

- CyberAgent Internet Surveillance: monitors websites, chat rooms, and bulletin boards 24/7 to identify trading or selling of personal information.

- Identity Theft Insurance: reimburses the individual for certain expenses in the event that his/her identity is compromised with a $1 million insurance policy.

- Court and Public Records Monitoring: identifies if individual's name, date of birth, and social security number appear in court records.

- Non-Credit Loan Monitoring: identifies if individual's personal information becomes linked to short-term, high-interest payday loans that don't require credit inquiries.

- Change of Address Monitoring: monitors to see if someone has redirected mail.

- Social Security Number Trace: identifies if a person's Social Security number becomes associated with another individual's name or address.

- Full-Service Identity Restoration: work with a certified identity theft restoration specialist to restore a person's identity if he or she experiences any fraud associated with his or her personal information.

Responses by Dr. Charles Romine

HOUSE COMMITTEE ON SCIENCE, SPACE, AND
TECHNOLOGY SUBCOMMITTEE ON RESEARCH AND
TECHNOLOGY SUBCOMMITTEE ON OVERSIGHT

"Is the OPM Data Breach the Tip of the Iceberg?"

Dr. Charles Romine, Director, Information Technology Laboratory, National Institute of
Standards and Technology

Questions submitted by Rep. Barbara Comstock, Chairwoman, Subcommittee on
Research and Technology and Rep. Barry Loudermilk, Chairman, Subcommittee on
Oversight

1. As you noted in your testimony, NIST creates baselines for minimum security requirements at federal agencies based on the importance of the information and information system to the mission of the agency. The requirements differ for each of the three categorization levels defined as low, moderate, and high. NIST also provides guidance to agencies to assist them in determining whether their established baseline is adequate to meet their risk-based requirements.

a. At what level is the OPM data for people's personally identifiable information- or PII - and information in clearance forms categorized?

RESPONSE: OPM does not report to NIST on its individual system and information categorization decisions. As noted in my testimony, FIPS 199 Information/System Categorization is done by the agency and reviewed by the Authorizing Official and the agency's Inspector General and subsequently reported to the Office of Management and Budget. Authorizing Officials and agency Risk Executives provide oversight of agency system categorizations.

b. How often did NIST staff meet with OPM staff to determine whether their established baseline is adequate to meet their risk-based requirements?

RESPONSE: NIST did not meet with OPM staff to discuss or determine if their established security control baseline was adequate to meet their mission requirements.

2. In your testimony, you "stress that the authorization of a system by a management official is an important quality control under FISMA. By authorizing processing in a system, the manager accepts the associated risk. This causes that official to formally assume responsibility for operating an information system at an acceptable level of risk to agency operations, agency assets, or individuals." Who is that manager or official at OPM?

RESPONSE: NIST does not receive information system authorization documentation, including the name of the authorizing official, for any system in the USG. You correctly state that the authorization to operate an agency information system is a critical quality control check. Each agency is responsible for developing and maintaining its system authorizations documents. The documentation required for a system authorization includes a System Security Plan, Security Assessment Report, and a Plan of Action and Milestones for any needed remediation, and the Authorization Decision. Risk assessment may be included in the authorization package. The authorization decision document should state the individual who authorized the system for operation, the terms and conditions for the authorization, and what residual risks are being accepted.

106

3. It appears that OPM had not encrypted some sensitive personal information that was compromised during the recent data breaches. What are the factors that agencies should consider when determining whether to encrypt sensitive information?

RESPONSE: There are several factors that agencies use in making decisions on the use of encryption to protect information. For moderate- and high-impact information and information systems, NIST security control SC-28, as defined in NIST guideline "Security and Privacy Controls for Federal Information Systems and Organizations," requires that agency information systems protect the confidentiality and/or integrity of agency-defined information at rest. Agencies can implement additional protective measures by employing the first control enhancement to SC-28 which states that agency information systems implement cryptographic mechanisms to prevent unauthorized disclosure and modification of agency-defined information on agency-defined information system components. Agencies also enhance their baseline security controls with a Risk Assessment looking at threat models, assets, and current vulnerabilities to establish prioritizations and increase protective measures if needed. Agencies can also examine current technologies and security architectures that are in use and available to them in implementing and monitoring security controls.

4. How often does NIST meet with and work with staff from federal agencies to help them establish their risk-based requirements?

a. Did NIST staff ever meet with OPM staff to discuss FISMA compliance?
b. If so, how often, and was this on par with the number of times NIST has met with other federal agencies?

RESPONSE: NIST meets bi-monthly with representatives from across the government through the Federal Computer Security Managers' Forum. The purpose of this forum, which is part of NIST's continuous improvement process, is to discuss NIST standards and guidelines, technologies and implementation challenges, receive feedback from stakeholders, and share lessons learned from across the government. NIST also has extensive outreach including visits to agencies, webinars, forums, workshops, email lists that provide education, training, and awareness for the technical content of our standards and guidelines. However, NIST does not provide guidance on specify agency solutions that an agency can obtain through the application of our standards and guidelines. Moreover, NIST does not adjudicate disagreements or disputes within agencies that could impact the risk-based decisions that are taken by agency heads in consultation with their professional staff. In that light, NIST staff has not met with OPM to discuss their FISMA compliance or specific risk-based solutions implemented by the agency.

5. In your testimony to the Committee, you emphasized the importance of collaboration with industry on lessons learned, cyber policy standards, and technology. As witnesses testified to the Committee, past efforts have mostly focused on the critical element of protecting against outside intrusions into our Federal networks. But we have also learned that once a breach occurs, the hackers have very few limitations on their ability to move within networks, thereby causing catastrophic damage.

a. In your collaboration with industry and best practices and technology, how are you vetting and developing policies around internal network standards to limit the breaches once they occur?

RESPONSE: NIST has produced guidance and recommendations, including *NIST SP 800-61r2, Computer Security Incident Handling Guide*, to limit the impact of a cybersecurity incident once it occurs. As with all of our guidance, NIST uses an inclusive and open process to engage industry, obtain feedback from the largest community possible, and provide accurate and effective recommendations to minimize impacts of cybersecurity incidents. NIST has developed specific contingency planning security controls and guidance in *NIST SP 800-53 Security and Privacy Controls for Federal Information Systems and Organizations* to assist with these incidents including such protective measures as system/domain isolation network segmentation, backup and recovery operations, malware containment.

b. What avenues does industry have to provide this type of input?

RESPONSE: Industry has multiple avenues to provide inputs to NIST. Through open workshops and conferences, individual meetings, public comments to draft standards and guidelines, collaboration on tools and reference materials, and participation in industry events and public private partnerships, NIST and industry maintain close contact to help ensure constant exchange of information.

108

HOUSE COMMITTEE ON SCIENCE, SPACE, AND
TECHNOLOGY SUBCOMMITTEE ON RESEARCH AND
TECHNOLOGY SUBCOMMITTEE ON OVERSIGHT

"Is the OPM Data Breach the Tip of the Iceberg?"

Dr. Charles Romine, Director, Information Technology Laboratory, National Institute of
Standards and Technology

Questions submitted by Rep. Eddie Bernice Johnson. Ranking Member, Committee on
Science, Space, and Technology

1. Under FISMA, NIST issues and updates security standards and guidelines for federal
information security systems. What is NIST's role in assisting other agencies with FISMA
implementation and compliance? Is there a process for federal agencies to reach out to NIST
to help them take advantage of NIST's technical expertise?

RESPONSE: NIST provides expertise, tools, briefings, and outreach to describe the existing
standards and guidelines that agencies use to implement and manage their information security
programs and comply with the requirements in FISMA. This outreach is required by FISMA.
Agencies can directly contact NIST program and project teams that developed the individual
standards and guidelines with questions, comments, and concerns. NIST also hosts a bi-monthly
Federal Computer Security Managers' Forum where agency information security officers meet
directly with NIST and agency peers to better understand NIST standards and guidelines, and
facilitate the sharing of best practices and lessons learned. Agencies also reach out to NIST
directly in the open public comment process, in the development of NIST standards and
guidelines, and in participation in NIST workshops and conferences.

2. FISMA requires the Department of Homeland Security's cybersecurity incident center
(US-CERT) to consult with NIST about information security incidents and other matters. Could
you please discuss that collaboration? Are there areas for improvement?

RESPONSE: NIST and US-CERT maintain a close collaboration on security incidents and other
matters. NIST and US-CERT closely collaborate in work on the National Vulnerability Database
(NVD). NIST creates and maintains standardized mechanisms to express vulnerabilities and
rapidly share vulnerability information and NIST-established vulnerability severity metrics. US-
CERT issues alerts, warnings, and advisories to the U.S. government using this data. This
partnership is currently very effective and includes regular meetings to ensure each organization
is supporting our respective missions and providing timely and meaningful information to federal
agencies. NIST and US-CERT are working jointly to ensure that, in the future, this information
can be created, shared, and acted upon as quickly as possible and to expand our audience. This
joint work involves improving existing specifications, creating new specifications, leveraging
newer technologies, and extending the National Vulnerability reference database to include new
technologies and provide improved access for the global community.

HOUSE COMMITTEE ON SCIENCE, SPACE, AND
TECHNOLOGY SUBCOMMITTEE ON RESEARCH AND
TECHNOLOGY SUBCOMMITTEE ON OVERSIGHT

"Is the OPM Data Breach the Tip of the Iceberg?"

Dr. Charles Romine, Director, Information Technology Laboratory, National Institute of
Standards and Technology

Questions submitted by Rep. Elizabeth Esty, Member, Subcommittee on Research and
Technology

1. The day after the hearing, the Office of Personnel Management (OPM) announced the
results of the investigation into the recent cyber-attack that involved the Federal background
investigation data. The investigation found that the security clearance background information
of 21.5 million individuals was compromised. Along with including significant information
about the individual (Social Security Numbers, current and former addresses, education
background, current and former employment information, financial information, travel
information, mental health information, criminal background, and substance use), the security
clearance background information form includes information about the individual's friends and
relatives and foreign contacts as well. Due to the extensive information included on the security
clearance background forms, I am concerned that standard credit monitoring is insufficient
protection. Please describe the kinds of protections that are needed to help protect individuals
who were compromised in this breach.

RESPONSE: NIST's role in cybersecurity is to provide standards and guidelines to help
federal agencies and other organizations protect their information and information systems.
We defer to other federal agencies whose missions include providing information and
resources to aid consumers and individuals, such as the Federal Trade Commission (and
IdentityTheft.gov) and the Consumer Financial Protection Board.

Appendix II

ADDITIONAL MATERIAL FOR THE RECORD

PREPARED STATEMENT OF COMMITTEE RANKING MEMBER
EDDIE BERNICE JOHSNON

Thank you Chairwoman Comstock and Chairman Loudermilk for holding this hearing on the recent OPM data breach.

Even though we will continue to learn more details about the breach, we already know that millions of Americans' personal information was compromised. This number includes current and retired federal employees as well as the family members, friends, and co-workers of federal employees.

There are valid concerns about hackers using this data for criminal purposes. Additionally, since security clearance background investigation information was compromised, there are also serious national security concerns.

It is frustrating to learn that OPM knew that they had serious information security systems problems long before this breach. Although addressing their information security systems is a top goal of the new OPM leadership, it is clear that action should have been taken years ago.

Federal computer information systems are guided by FISMA. In this risk management approach, agencies evaluate the type of data in their systems, determine what level of controls are needed, and put together a plan to adequately protect their data.

Although NIST is responsible for drafting the standards used by the agencies, they do not oversee the program and are not responsible for enforcing agency compliance with FISMA.

Instead of picking on one federal agency, it is my hope that we can use this data breach as a starting point for addressing federal cybersecurity more broadly. What is working? What is not? What mechanisms need to be in place to better protect individuals' personal information on our federal systems?

I want to end by saying that any conversation about federal cybersecurity must include a discussion about resources. It would be irresponsible for us to mandate additional cybersecurity measures that federal agencies must take without providing them with additional resources.

Cybersecurity will always be about managing risks. No information security system, whether public sector or private sector, can be completely protected. And unfortunately the question is, when, not if a system will get hacked. Therefore, we must ensure that we have the appropriate policies and oversight in place to help federal agencies protect their data, and that we have provided federal agencies with the resources they need to do the job effectively.

I want to thank the witnesses for their testimony and I yield back the balance of my time.

UNITED STATES OFFICE OF PERSONNEL MANAGEMENT
Washington, DC 20415

Office of the
Inspector General

June 17, 2015

MEMORANDUM FOR KATHERINE ARCHULETA
         Director

FROM: PATRICK E. McFARLAND
         Inspector General

SUBJECT: Flash Audit Alert – U.S. Office of Personnel Management's
         Infrastructure Improvement Project (Report No. 4A-CI-00-15-055)

Executive Summary

The U.S. Office of Personnel Management (OPM) Office of the Inspector General (OIG) is issuing this Flash Audit Alert to bring to your immediate attention serious concerns we have regarding the Office of the Chief Information Officer's (OCIO) infrastructure improvement project (Project).[1] This Project includes a full overhaul of the agency's technical infrastructure by implementing additional information technology (IT) security controls and then migrating the entire infrastructure into a completely new environment (referred to as Shell).

Our primary concern is that the OCIO has not followed U.S. Office of Management and Budget (OMB) requirements and project management best practices. The OCIO has initiated this project without a complete understanding of the scope of OPM's existing technical infrastructure or the scale and costs of the effort required to migrate it to the new environment.

In addition, we have concerns with the nontraditional Government procurement vehicle that was used to secure a sole-source contract with a vendor to manage the infrastructure overhaul. While we agree that the sole-source contract may have been appropriate for the initial phases of securing the existing technical environment, we do not agree that it is appropriate to use this vehicle for the long-term system migration efforts.

We intend to conduct further oversight of this Project and may issue additional reports in the future. However, we have identified substantial issues requiring immediate action, and we are therefore issuing the following recommendations in this Flash Audit Alert, so that the OCIO can immediately begin taking steps to address these concerns. We provided a draft of this Alert to the OCIO for their review, but we did not receive any comments.

---

[1] This audit report has been distributed to Federal officials who are responsible for the administration of the audited program. This audit report may contain proprietary data which is protected by Federal law (18 U.S.C. 1905). Therefore, while this audit report is available under the Freedom of Information Act and made available to the public on the OIG webpage (http://www.opm.gov/our-inspector-general), caution needs to be exercised before releasing the report to the general public as it may contain proprietary information that was redacted from the publicly distributed copy.

1) **Project Management Activities**

We were told that OPM officials initiated the Project to improve the security of its network and operating environment after learning of a significant security incident in March 2014. The initial plan was to make major security improvements to the existing environment and continue to operate OPM systems in their current location. During the process of implementing security upgrades, OPM determined that it would be more effective to completely overhaul the agency's IT infrastructure and architecture and move it into a completely new environment.

The new plan involves hosting OPM systems in two commercial data centers. The new architecture will be a distributed computing environment, with no mainframe or legacy applications. We have been told by OCIO officials that no applications will be allowed to migrate to the new Shell environment unless they are rebuilt to be compatible with all new security and operating features of the new architecture. The phases of this Project include Tactical (shoring up the existing security environment), Shell (creating the new data center and IT architecture), Migration (migrating all OPM systems to the new architecture), and Cleanup (decommissioning existing hardware and systems). The current status is that the Tactical phase is complete, and the Shell phase is underway.

While we agree in principle that this is an ideal future goal for the agency's IT environment, we have serious concerns regarding OPM's management of this Project. The Project is already underway and the agency has committed substantial funding, but it has not yet addressed several critical project management requirements, including, but not limited to:

- OPM has not yet identified the full scope and cost of this project;
- OPM has not prepared a 'Major IT Business Case' (formerly known as the OMB Exhibit 300), as required by OMB for IT projects of this size and scope; and,
- OPM's overall project management process is missing a number of critical artifacts considered to be best practices by relevant organizations.

As a result, there is a high risk that this Project will fail to meet the objectives of providing a secure operating environment for OPM systems and applications.

Many critical OPM applications (including those that process annuity payments for Federal retirees, reimburse health insurance companies for claims payments, and manage background investigations) run on OPM's mainframe computers. These applications are based on legacy technology, and will need to be completely renovated to be compatible with OPM's proposed new IT architecture.

To help put this in perspective, we reference OPM's Fiscal Year (FY) 2009 efforts to migrate a single financial system application from the mainframe. This project was relatively well managed and was subject to oversight from several independent entities, including the OIG, but it still required two years and over $30 million to complete. OPM's current initiative is much more massive than this prior project, as each individual application migration should

115

be treated as its own project similar to this example. Furthermore, there are many other systems besides OPM's mainframe applications that will also need to be modified to some extent to be compatible.

The Migration phase of this Project will clearly be a complex, expensive, and lengthy process. OPM currently estimates that it will take 18 to 24 months to complete. We believe this is overly optimistic and that the agency is highly unlikely to meet this target. In fact, OPM is still in the process of evaluating its existing IT architecture, including the identification of all mainframe applications that will need to be migrated, and other systems that will need to be redesigned. OCIO representatives are currently conducting a compatibility assessment for the "major OPM investments" as encompassed by three program offices: Retirement Services, Federal Investigative Services, and Human Resources Solutions. It was explained to us that this review only addresses approximately 80 percent of OPM's systems, with the remainder considered out of scope for this evaluation, but to be eventually addressed. This assessment is not scheduled for completion until next month (July 2015). It is difficult to see how the agency can estimate its timeline when it does not yet know the scope of the effort.

Related to the unknown scope of the Project is the uncertainty of its overall cost. OPM has estimated that the Tactical and Shell phases of the Project will cost approximately $93 million. OMB has included $21 million in the President's FY 2016 budget to fund part of this amount. Another $5 million was contributed by the Department of Homeland Security to support its continuous monitoring program, and the remaining $67 million is being collected from OPM's major program offices as a special assessment. However, this estimate does not include the costs to migrate the many existing applications to the new IT environment, which are likely to be substantial.

When we asked about the funding for the Migration phase, we were told, in essence, that OPM would find the money somehow, and that program offices would be required to fund the migration of applications that they own from their existing budgets. However, program office budgets are intended to fund OPM's core operations, not subsidize a major IT infrastructure project. It is unlikely that OPM will be able to fund the substantial migration costs related to this Project without a significantly adverse impact on its mission, unless it seeks dedicated funding through Congressional appropriation. Also, OPM's current budget approach seems to violate IT spending transparency principles promoted by OMB's budget guidance and its IT Dashboard initiative, which is intended to "shine [a] light onto the performance and spending of IT investments across the Federal Government."

In addition to the undefined scope and uncertain budget, OPM has not completed other standard, and critical, project management steps. Control Objectives for Information and Related Technology (COBIT) is a framework created by the Information System Audit and Control Association (ISACA) for IT management and IT governance. The Committee of Sponsoring Organizations of the Treadway Commission (COSO) framework also identifies internal controls required for effective organizational management.

COBIT and the COSO framework define best practices for major IT developments. Several examples of critical processes that OPM has not completed for this project include:

- Project charter;
- Comprehensive list of project stakeholders;
- Feasibility study to address scope and timeline in concert with budgetary justification/cost estimates;
- Impact assessment for existing systems and stakeholders;
- Quality assurance plan and procedures for contractor oversight;
- Technological infrastructure acquisition plan;
- High-level test plan; and,
- Implementation plan to include resource planning, readiness assessment plan, success factors, conversion plan, and back-out plan.

In our opinion, the project management approach for this major infrastructure overhaul is entirely inadequate, and introduces a very high risk of project failure. The correct approach would be to use the OMB budget process to request project funding using the OMB-required Major IT Business Case (Exhibit 300) process. This would require OPM to fully evaluate the costs, benefits, and risks associated with its planned Project, and present its business case to OMB to seek approval and funding.

OMB Circular A-11 Appendix 6 defines capital budgeting requirements for capital asset projects. The basic concepts are that capital asset projects require proper planning, cost/benefit analysis, financing, and risk management. This includes demonstrating that the return on investment exceeds the cost of funds used, and an analysis of the "investment's total life-cycle costs and benefits, including the total budget authority required for the asset..."

Furthermore, the financing principles outlined in the Circular state that "Good budgeting requires that appropriations for the full cost of asset acquisition be enacted in advance to help ensure that all costs and benefits are fully taken into account at the time decisions are made to provide resources."

Finally, the Circular requires risk management and earned value management throughout the life-cycle of the project: "The investment cost, schedule, and performance goals established through the Planning Phase of the investment are the basis for approval to procure the asset and the basis for assessing risk. During the Procurement Phase, performance-based management systems (earned value management system) must be used to provide contractor and Government management visibility on the achievement of, or deviation from, goals until the asset is accepted and operational."

OMB's FY 2016 IT Budget – Capital Planning Guidance further states that "Together, the Major IT Business Cases and Major IT Business Case Details provide the budgetary and management information necessary for sound planning, management, and governance of IT investments. These documents help agencies explicitly align IT investments with strategic and performance goals, and ultimately provide value to the public by making investment and management information more transparent." OMB expects that artifacts, documents, and associated data similar to those defined by the COBIT and COSO frameworks already exist when a Major IT Business Case is submitted as part of an agency's budget process.

OPM officials informed us that the urgent and compelling nature of the situation required immediate action, and this is the reason that some of the required project management activities were not completed. We agree with and support the agency's efforts to improve its IT security infrastructure through the Tactical phase of this Project. We understand and accept that immediate action was required and that it was appropriate to do so. However, the other phases of the project are clearly going to require long-term effort, and, to be successful, will require the disciplined processes associated with proper system development project management.

Without these disciplined processes, there is a high risk that this Project will fail to meet all of its stated objectives. In addition, without a guaranteed source of funding in place, OPM may not have the internal resources necessary to complete the Migration phase, which is likely to be complex and expensive. In this scenario, the agency would be forced to indefinitely support multiple data centers, further stretching already inadequate resources, possibly making both environments less secure, and increasing costs to taxpayers. This outcome would be contrary to the stated goals of creating a more secure IT environment at a lower cost.

Recommendation 1

We recommend that OPM's OCIO complete an OMB Major IT Business Case document as part of the FY 2017 budget process and submit this document to OMB for approval. Associated with this effort, the OCIO should complete its assessment of the scope of the migration process, the level of effort required to complete it, and its estimated costs. Furthermore, the OCIO should implement the project management processes required by OMB and recommended by ISACA's COBIT and the COSO framework.

2) Sole-Source Contract

OPM has secured a sole-source contract with a vendor to manage the infrastructure improvement project from start to finish. Although OPM completed a Justification for Other Than Full and Open Competition (JOFOC) to justify this contract, we do not agree that it is appropriate to use this contract for the entire Project.

The initial phase of the Project covered the procurement, installation, and configuration of a variety of software tools designed to improve the IT security posture of the agency (the Tactical phase). We agree that recent security breaches at OPM warranted a thorough and immediate reaction to secure the existing environment, and that the JOFOC was appropriate for this tactical activity.

However, the JOFOC also covered subsequent phases of the Project related to the development of the new Shell infrastructure, the migration of all of OPM's applications into this new environment, and decommissioning the old environment. Although the Shell phase is largely complete, there is still an opportunity to procure contractor support for the migration and cleanup phases of this project using the appropriate contracting vehicles. Without submitting this Project to an open competition, OPM has no benchmark to evaluate whether the costs charged by the sole-source vendor are reasonable and appropriate.

As stated previously, we expect the Migration phase to be extremely complex and time consuming. It will likely require significant contractor support, with each application requiring a unique skill set. OPM may also determine that it would benefit from a contractor to oversee the Migration effort as a whole. We believe that contractor support for both application-specific migration and the Migration and Cleanup efforts as a whole are not justifiably covered by the existing sole-source contract. FAR 6.302 outlines seven scenarios where contracting without full and open competition may be appropriate, two of which relate to an unusual and compelling urgency and national security implications. However, we have not been provided evidence that the Migration and Cleanup phases of this project meet the FAR criteria for bypassing an open competition.

We believe that OPM should gain a complete and thorough understanding of the scope of this Project, request funding from OMB via the appropriate avenues (See Recommendation 1) and *then* subject the remainder of the project to contracting vehicles other than the sole source contract used for the Tactical and Shell phases.

Recommendation 2

We recommend that OPM not leverage its existing sole source contract for the Migration and Cleanup phases of the infrastructure improvement project. Contractor support for these phases should be procured using existing contracts already supporting legacy information systems or via full and open competition.

If you have any questions about this Flash Audit Alert you can contact me, at 606-1200, or your staff may wish to contact Michael R. Esser, Assistant Inspector General for Audits, at 606-2143.

cc: Chris Canning
       Acting Chief of Staff

       Angela Bailey
       Chief Operating Officer

       Janet Barnes
       Director, Internal Oversight and Compliance

       Donna K. Seymour
       Chief Information Officer

http://blogs.fedsmith.com/2015/06/25/feds-demand-communication-from-obama-on-data-breach/

June 25, 2015

President Barack Obama
The White House
1600 Pennsylvania Avenue, N.W.
Washington, D.C. 20500

Dear Mr. President:

The undersigned organizations of the Federal-Postal Coalition, which collectively represent five million federal and postal workers, retirees and their survivors, write to express our deep concern over the failure of the federal government to adequately protect its personnel computer systems and the devastating impact recent breaches of these systems may have on tens of millions of Americans, including the federal workforce.

Along with all Americans, we are profoundly disturbed by the acknowledgment by government officials that state or non-state actors have stolen massive numbers of personnel records maintained by the Office of Personnel Management (OPM), including highly personal and sensitive security clearance data of millions of current and former employees, and even applicants for federal employment. These breaches could give our enemies the means to attempt to corrupt or blackmail government employees to spy or compromise military and intelligence secrets, and even to attempt to recruit Americans to join or assist terrorist organizations. Moreover, they could lead to the possibility that particular public servants – including intelligence, diplomacy and development, law enforcement, prosecutorial, and defense civilian personnel – could become vulnerable to grave risks that threaten their personal security and that of their families and loved ones.

Government employees reasonably expect their employer to faithfully protect the sensitive information they are required to disclose as a condition of their employment. But the long history of systemic failure by OPM and other agencies to properly manage their information technology infrastructure (IT) has undermined that expectation. Despite the explicit warnings by inspectors general since 1997 to OPM to take all necessary steps to guard its aged and newer computer systems, the agency has acted or failed to act in ways that have permitted the theft of massive amounts of personally identifiable information. As recently as last week, the Inspector General of OPM issued a flash audit of OPM's plans to improve its data security and found them to have a "very high risk of project failure."

The responsibility to correct what has transpired and to put the nation on a new course rests with you as the Chief Executive. This involves greater communication with federal workers and retirees, the organizations that represent them, and others impacted; heightened accountability; and the application of more aggressive safeguards to protect federal IT systems, including workforce databases.

To date, federal leaders have shared woefully insufficient information with the federal workforce, retirees and the American people about the breaches that have occurred, the extent of information revealed and what measures are being taken to prevent further harm. More meaningful and timely communication with those affected is critical. In addition, the financial credit reporting measures OPM has offered to those whose information has been compromised are woefully inadequate. We urge you to mandate immediate measures that inform federal employees, former employees and others whether their personal information has been disclosed through the breach of federal personnel and security clearance systems, and provide them with long-term credit protection measures.

The challenge of overhauling the legacy and current federal personnel systems to assure their protection also requires intensive effort. As you did with Healthcare.gov, we call upon you to immediately appoint a task force of leading agency, defense/intelligence, and private-sector IT experts, with a short deadline, to assist in the ongoing investigation, apply more forceful measures to protect federal personnel IT systems, and assure adequate notice to the federal workforce and the American public. The task force should be responsible for rebuilding the government's personnel databases to ensure their protection and functionality to the greatest extent possible. The gravity of the situation necessitates the full attention of the Administration and the leadership involvement of your top technology officials.

We also call upon you to request supplementary appropriations to ensure that these aims are fulfilled as quickly as possible. Time is not on our side; we do not have years to wait for OPM to complete this task on its own.

Our nation will remain strong because its people and its government are resolute in their commitment to the preservation of its security. We cannot allow the government's IT practices of the past to continue. The recent breaches are a wake-up call to this country and its leaders about the dangers of cyberterrorism and the critical need to protect our government's core functions. We ask you to apply the highest priority to these concerns in continuing to keep our country safe.

Thank you for your time and consideration of our views. Questions related to this communication should be directed to Alan Lopatin, Chairman of the Federal-Postal Coalition, at 202-487-4800 or Alan@ledgecounsel.com.

Sincerely,

American Federation of Government Employees

American Federation of State, County and Municipal Employees

American Foreign Service Association

FAA Managers Association

Federal Managers Association

Federally Employed Women

International Association of Fire Fighters

Laborers' International Union of North America

National Active and Retired Federal Employees Association

National Air Traffic Controllers Association

National Association of Assistant United States Attorneys

National Association of Government Employees

National Association of Letter Carriers

National Association of Postal Supervisors

National Association of Postmasters of the United States

National Council of Social Security Management Associations

National Federation of Federal Employees

National League of Postmasters

National Postal Mail Handlers Union

National Rural Letter Carriers' Association

National Treasury Employees Union

National Weather Service Employees Organization

Organization of Professional Employees at the U.S. Dept. of Agriculture

Patent Office Professional Association

Professional Aviation Safety Specialists

Professional Managers Association

Senior Executives Association

www.ingramcontent.com/pod-product-compliance
Lightning Source LLC
LaVergne TN
LVHW060144070326
832902LV00018B/2946